Eastern Coyote Challenge

Andrew L. Lewand

Copyright 2009
Andrew L. Lewand

ISBN: 1448602866
EAN-13: 9781448602865

Published by **LEWAND OUTDOORS**
Cover Design: Craig Sleeman

No part of this book may be copied or reproduced without the written permission of the author.

Dedication

I dedicate this book to my parents, Richard and Janice Lewand, for their love and support over the years.

Table of Contents

Introduction 5

Chapter 1	Getting to Know the Eastern Coyote	9
Chapter 2	Equipment; Gear, calls, guns...........................	23
Chapter 3	Obtaining Permission	45
Chapter 4	Perfect Practice day and night	51
Chapter 5	Factors for Success	59
Chapter 6	Calling to Coyotes	81
Chapter 7	Be a Storyteller	89
Chapter 8	Bring on the Night	91
Chapter 9	Three Season Calling	115
Chapter 10	Two Timing Coyotes	127
Chapter 11	Stubborn Coyotes	133
Chapter 12	After the shot	139
Chapter 13	Hunter Resources	143

Appendix.. 147

Introduction

The coyote (Canis Latrans) has received more than its share of publicity in recent times. He has been blamed for the decline in the deer take in many northeastern states. He has been viewed as a ravenous killer of all things wild. He is also viewed as one of the most adaptable animals on the face of the earth, showing the ability to live almost anywhere. While the coyote has been expanding its range since the turn of the century, its presence in the northeastern states has been truly noticeable since the late 1980's.

It was 1983 when I first came across the Eastern coyote. I was a second-year college student, majoring in Fish and Wildlife Technology at the State University of New York at Cobleskill. My field assignment was to monitor coyote den sites. Mind you, this was a time before trail cameras came into vogue. Those were some long hours as we waited, hiding in tall grass and swatting mosquitoes, to catch a glimpse of our study subject. The wait became worthwhile when an adult coyote trotted across an open pasture with a rabbit in its mouth, as it headed back to the den. Instantly, I found myself drawn to the charisma of the coyote.

In 1984, my interest with the coyote took a new turn. It happened as I was engaged in a morning woodchuck hunt in central New York. It was a banner morning as nine woodchucks succumbed to my Remington 700 in 223. However, that was not the highlight. Just as the hunt was about to end, my Father spotted a large canine running across the field. I saw it just in time to identify it as a coyote. "You can call those in, you know," My father stated. Our excitement ran high, and we went out to the nearest sporting goods store to purchase a mouth call. That same afternoon, we were right back in the field, armed with our new wooden cottontail rabbit distress call. Within a minute of blowing the call, a coyote appeared in the field. It was a young coyote, and we did not shoot at it. What we did was realize that coyotes were taking a stronghold in our area, and that they could be hunted using this exciting technique!

These two encounters paved the way to a personal 33-plus year fascination with the coyote. I'm glad to know that I'm not alone. The fact that you are reading this book indicates that you have an interest in coyotes, as well. The focus of this book shall be on gaining an understanding of how to be more successful in calling and killing Eastern coyotes. Before I continue, I want to announce that I admire, respect and value coyotes. Like all living things, they have a deserved place in the ecosystem. This being said, I am also truly passionate about pursuing them as a game species.

While giving predator hunting seminars, I make a point of telling the attendees that, regardless of their experience level, something they hear or see in the presentation will help them become a more successful hunter. I feel the same about the contents of this book. Whether you have been calling coyotes for two months, or twenty years, you are sure to pick up some tips and knowledge within these pages that well assist you in putting more fur in your truck.

Although the book focuses on calling Eastern coyotes, there is little doubt that the information can be applied to coyotes living anywhere in North America. The chapters are organized so that the book is a comprehensive guide to successful calling and the information is instructional and often presented in a "how to" fashion. In effort to capture the true essence of coyote calling, I have related personal hunting experiences throughout the text. These anecdotes highlight what can go right during and hunt and surely… what can go wrong.

The book contains segments entitled "At the Next Level" that provide more than the basics of the sport. Indeed, I have included advanced strategies, tips, and techniques in each chapter that will make hunters of all experience levels more successful

Writing this book has been a labor of love and reinforced how much I enjoy coyote hunting. This book was originally published in 2009. In 2017, I decided to re-visit the text and see if it needed refreshing. I realized that the tactics that worked in 2009 still work today. Hence, that information could stay intact. Any new calling strategies and tactics that I have experienced since, and there have been a lot, have been included in several of my other predator hunting books that I have released over the years.

One area of content that did seem dated was the section on night hunting. More specifically, the options of scanning and shooting lights that are available to today's hunters. The way the sport is evolving, it may be impossible to keep up with what manufacturers are providing. Surely, it is an exciting time to be a predator hunter.

For a period of time, when I was completing the book, I was either calling to coyotes or writing about it. Those were good days! With that being said, I hope you enjoy *Eastern Coyote Challenge!*

Andrew L. Lewand
Summer 2017

An Eastern coyote stands guard over his territory.

Chapter 1

Getting to know the Eastern Coyote

While an entire book could be written on the subject of coyote biology and ecology, I feel it is important, at least, to devote a chapter on the subject in this book. The reasoning is simple: The more a hunter knows about his quarry, and the better he understands it, the better his success at hunting it. The biological information is presented to assist hunters in becoming more familiar with the Eastern coyote. This knowledge will lay a foundation for the calling techniques and strategies that are discussed throughout the subsequent chapters in the book.

Physical Appearance

I'll start with a question: While driving along, have you ever spotted a canine trotting across a field and turned your truck around at the nearest driveway to take another look at the critter – only to find out that it was actually a farm dog? If you answered "yes" there is no need for embarrassment. I've done it on several occasions.

Indeed, the Eastern coyote does resemble a Shepherd in size and shape. Perhaps the best way to differentiate the two, from a distance, is to notice the tail. If it is carried low, at a downward angle, the critter is likely a coyote. Conversely, domestic dogs typically carry their tails in an upwardly curled position.

The Eastern coyote (Photo courtesy of PGC/Billie Cromwell)

The adult Eastern coyote's body weight varies from between 30 and 60 pounds. There are two basic reasons why Eastern coyotes are so much heavier than their Western counterparts. First, DNA testing has shown that Northeastern Coyotes have been hybridized with both red wolves from the southern states and gray wolves from the Northern regions. This hybridization left a genetically larger animal. The second reason for the large body weight of Eastern coyotes is the evolutionary adaption to consuming larger prey species. In many locales, the Eastern coyote's diet features the whitetail deer. Coyotes in these areas, throughout time, have developed into larger and heavier animals because that is what is necessary to take down the deer. Reports of 60 pound coyotes surface regularly, and I'm not one to dispute them.

The coloration of Eastern coyotes is varied. By some accounts, there are said to be over 30 color variations on coyotes. Again, this can be most likely attributed to cross-breeding. Coyotes can appear as blonde, gray, brown, black and almost any color scheme in between. The coyote coat is made of two layers; an undercoat for insulation and longer guard hairs to act as first defense against the elements. Typically, the tail is bushy and features a black tip. On rare occasions, coyotes may have a white-tipped tail.

Coyote Senses

The coyote is ever cautious. In order to survive in the wild, the coyote needs to rely on all of its senses. Luckily for the coyote, all of its senses are highly developed. Let's take a quick look at the coyote's abilities to see, smell and hear.

Vision

Coyotes have excellent vision... for their needs. They have excellent visual ability in low light situations and can detect the slightest of movements. In daylight, coyotes see well, but their visual clarity is not the best at far distances. In fact, they may be considered near sighted. A coyote's night vision is his strong point. Why is this? Both the human and canine eye consists of cells called rods and cones. Rods are more useful for night vision and cones are more suited for day vision. Humans have more cones than rod cells in the eyes. As a result, we are better suited for day vision. Coyotes have a high percentage of rod cells; hence they have enhanced night vision.

The two most commonly asked questions among curious hunters are... "Are coyotes colorblind?" and "Why doesn't the red light bother predators at night?" The answer is that coyotes are not completely color blind. However, they do not have the same color vision as humans. This occurs because coyotes have only two color receptors in their eyes, whereas humans have three. Coyotes can see the blue colors, but not red. They see the color red as a dull yellow. At night, coyotes see their world as shades of gray.

Smell

The coyote's nose may be his best ally. The long snout of a coyote is lined with millions of scent receptors and the coyote is able to smell odors in parts per trillion, as opposed to humans who smell in parts per thousand. Coyotes will most often use their sense of smell when approaching a feeding situation. The process of "circling down wind" to detect foreign odors helps coyotes avoid dangerous situations. There is a school of thought that says the Eastern coyotes rely on their acute sense of smell even more than coyotes from other regions. Perhaps it is due to the thick vegetation or hilly terrain that limits their ability to see for long distances. Or, perhaps, it is the living in such close proximity to humans. Whatever the case, Eastern coyotes use their sense of smell to their advantage. We, as hunters, must learn to use this knowledge to our advantage if we are to have success while calling them in.

Hearing

The coyote's ability to hear is as sharp as his other senses. Their hearing is said to be twice that of humans. The three parts of a coyote's ear help explain its excellent hearing. Their large forward facing ears (external ear) help pin-point sound and help determine exactly where the sound is coming from. The middle ear amplifies the sound, and the internal ear converts sound vibrations to nerve impulses for the brain to interpret. The combination of excellent hearing, sense of smell and vision creates a critter that is well equipped to survive in a variety of conditions.

What about "Coydogs"?

Years back, when I first started asking people landowners to hunt their farms for coyotes, I would often hear... "We don't have coyotes, but we do have those coy-dogs." That was fine by me. I just wanted to call something in! As it turned out, I never called in any of their coydogs, but I did shoot a few coyotes.

Coydogs are something of a mystery to most folks. The fact is that they can and do exist. It is possible for a domestic dog to mate with a wild coyote. However, for several reasons they don't seem to last too long in the wild. First off, hybrid females give birth in the early winter months of November or December. This means that the pups would be born in January or February and the weather conditions would be far too harsh for pup survival. Additionally, male coydogs do not assist with rearing of the young. This causes too much burden on the female for successful rearing. The coydog litters are much smaller than wild coyote litters. Because pup survival is so low, even for wild coyotes, small litters will result in lower survival numbers for the pups. Coydogs have another thing going against them. Compared to wild coyotes, coydogs are not competitive in nature. This simply means that they cannot compete for survival in the wild. All of these drawbacks mean one thing for coydogs in the wild... successive generations die out.

Coyote Diet

Part of the coyote's success at survival and range expansion is its ability to adapt to various living situations. The wide variety of items that make up the coyote's diet is part of this adaptability. The coyote is an opportunistic feeder, meaning that it will feed on what is available. The list of items on the coyote's menu consist of, but is not limited to, grasses, fruits, insects, mice, voles, squirrels, rabbits, birds and deer. Coyotes will eat carrion and basically whatever else is available. I have witnessed coyotes eating leftover Burger King French fries on a dead-end road and dog food from my neighbor's dog bowl.

Regarding deer predation, the impact of coyotes on the deer population is a subject of great debate. Deer hunters who experience ᴸower deer sightings are quick to blame the coyote. I am aware of one recent study that showed that, through coyote scat analysis, deer comprise 50-70% of coyote diet in June/July. Furthermore, analysis of the bone marrow in coyote killed deer indicated that the deer where healthy when killed. This fact debunks the notion that coyotes only kill sick, weak and old deer.

Reproduction and Denning

The mating season for Eastern coyotes typically occurs in January and February. During this time, a female comes into heat for 3-4 days. A group of lone males will gather to the female and vie for her affection. I first saw this process a few years back and it was most interesting. At first, I did not realize what has happening. It was a January morning and I was attempting to make a mid-morning stand. As I approached the field, I spotted a "pack" of 5 coyotes already in the field. Due to the sparseness of the terrain, I could only watch them from a distance of 500 yards. Through my binoculars, I saw them leap-frogging, rolling, and spinning around. They appeared to be having a grand time. At times, one coyote would simply lie down and watch the mayhem. I attempted to call them in, but they were too content with their business. They frolicked for a solid 20 minutes an eventually drifted away. As I drove to a new farm, it dawned on me as to what I had just witnessed…. coyote courtship!

Through this process, the female picks one lucky male coyote and they will mate. The mated female will prepare up to 12 separate dens.

14

These dens will often be made on hillsides, banks, under fallen logs or in thickets. The den entrances often face south to allow the sun to warm the den. Many times, they are often enlarged woodchuck dens.

After a gestation period of 63-65 days, the pups will be born. The average litter size is 5-7 pups and the litter size depends upon food availability. In years when food is readily available, the litter sizes will be larger. The opposite is conversely true. Older female coyotes will give birth to larger litters than younger females. Females will only have 1 litter per year. A "double litter" occurs when a younger female cannot find suitable den territory and shares a den with another female, typically her mother.

Females will nurse pups for 6 weeks. Solid food is eaten when pups are 4 weeks old and male coyotes assist the females by bring food back for her and the young. The male coyote does not frequently use the den himself. Pups can walk by 3 weeks and will run by 4 weeks of age. Pups gain independence by July and August and will roam to explore their surroundings in areas called rendezvous sites. The family unit stays together through the early fall. Pups will disperse from October through January. The dispersal distances vary from 5 to 50 miles. One radio-collared coyote in New York State was found to travel 150 miles. It has been noted that the family units stay together longer in the Northeast than in other areas of the country.

Daily Movement and Home Range

Many people are not aware that they are living in such close proximity to coyotes. That is because Eastern coyotes will use the cover of darkness and vegetation to their advantage. Eastern coyotes are most active and travel the farthest distance between 6 PM and 6 AM. This nocturnal time slot works well for coyotes as this is when their food sources are moving, and they can go undetected as they hunt. It has been found that females travel the farthest distance per day and that the average daily distances traveled was the least in Autumn and greatest in winter. This makes sense if you consider availability and ease of obtaining food. Daily movements are greatest during the breeding period and female travel distances decreased during nursing while males increased. Again, this makes sense as you consider what the coyotes are up to during these times.

Home ranges for Eastern coyotes are larger than those of western coyotes. This is due to food availability. As a general statement, a female's home range is approximately 6 square miles while a male's can expand to 40 square miles. Home ranges can increase during May – June and decrease from July – December. A breeding pair's home range, in January/February, will be that of the female: 6 miles.

Sounds of the Coyote

Coyotes do something that most other animals do not do… They make signature noises throughout the entire year. The sound most often associated with coyotes is their howl. While some folks think the sound is eerie or frightening, to the coyote hunter it is a glorious and almost always welcome sound. Although coyotes can most often be heard howling near dusk and dawn, they can and do howl at any hour. Mid-day fire whistles have been known to illicit packs of coyotes to sound off in apparent response.

Coyotes howl for a variety of reasons and communication is the primary goal. They will howl to locate their pack members. They will howl to locate their pack members. They will also howl to other coyote packs to announce their presence and for territorial rights.

Coyotes will howl to members of the opposite sex during the mating season as they search for a mate. Coyotes have also been observed howling for no apparent reason at all. Perhaps these coyotes are simply trying to live up to their common nick-name: The Song Dog!

Research shows that there are times of the year when coyotes are more vocal. A spike in howling frequency has been noted during the month of November and again during February. This can be attributed to times of pup dispersal and coyotes are sounding off for territorial purpose and also during the mating season when coyotes are searching for mates.

A coyote emits a lone howl to find a mate.

The hunter should acquaint himself with the various types of howls that are most frequently heard while afield. It may be best to learn each sound by having an experienced coyote caller demonstrate the sound. It is also possible to find the sounds on the internet and listen to them there. When using the internet, there is one word of caution, however. Be sure to cross-reference the sounds as they may be incorrectly labeled. The misuse of these sounds could result in less than favorable results while hunting. With an actual understanding of these sounds, the hunter will be better equipped to deal with vocal coyotes when hunting them.

The Group Howl: A group of coyotes howling in concert creates quite a ruckus. When two or more coyotes start howling together, the sound is intriguing to say the least. It often sounds as if far many more coyotes are creating the sound. I frequently hear from landowners, "The coyotes were howling out back last night and there must have been a dozen of them." The numbers are usually far less, as two coyotes can end up sounding like four and so on. In any event, a group howl can indicate that coyotes are sounding off to let their position be known to other coyotes. Pack members can find each other as they travel during the night through the group howl. Rival packs will be aware of resident coyote territories through the use of group howls. In either case, the group howl announces the coyote's presence and that is useful information to coyote hunters.

The Lone Howl: A solitary howl is another example of communication between coyotes. This long, drawn out howl can be made by any coyote regardless of gender or age. In mating time, a female could howl to summons a male and vice versa. As coyotes are highly territorial, a lone howl from a coyote could result in dominate coyotes venturing over to see just who is invading his turf. Hunters can take advantage of this type of communication; this will be discussed in forthcoming chapters.

The Challenge Bark/Howl: This type of communication is characterized by a few crisp barks that precede a wavering howl. Coyotes emit the challenge bark when they know that something is amiss in their environment. Whether it is meant as a warning to other coyotes or to whatever has caused the concern, the challenge howling coyote means business. The sequence is often repeated until the threat is gone. Again, strategies for dealing with challenge barking coyotes will be discussed in forthcoming chapters.

Track Analysis

Tell-tale sign of deer, turkey or canine prints in snow or dirt are the essence of scouting. The presence of such sign is a sure-fire indicator that animals are using the area. While deer and turkey tracks are easily recognizable from other animal tracks, coyote tracks are often confused with other canines that may also be using the area. In determining if the track in question is indeed a coyote, the observer should first analyze the basic shape and size of the track. An adult coyote's print will be 2 inches wide by 2.5 inches long and will feature the two middle toes pointed together. A domestic dog print will feature toe prints that splay outward. A fox print will be more oval in shape and much smaller than that of a coyote.

Coyotes Tracks   *Domestic Dog Tracks*

Tracks like these are sure indicators that coyotes are using an area.

There are some tricks to analyzing the tracks in the snow as well. Due to a coyote's relatively narrow chest cavity, the right-side paw prints and left side paw prints will be closer together, as they leave tracks in snow or mud, than a domestic dog's prints. As a result, the coyote paw prints appear to be in line with each other. A domestic dog, with its wider chest cavity, will leave prints that form a "zigzag" pattern in snow or mud.

There is also something to be gained by observing the travel pathway that the tracks make in the snow. As a general rule, the coyote's pathway will appear more as a straight line. In comparison, a domestic dog's pathway will be a random path featuring many twists and turns.

Population Dynamics

We shall finish our coyote ecology discussion with a look at population dynamics. The numbers associated with Eastern coyote age structure and mortality are often surprising. The sex ratio is typically balanced between males and females. In areas with higher coyote densities, more males will be born. When coyote populations are stressed, more females will be born into each litter.

Life in the wild is hard on coyotes, and old coyotes are hard to come by. In fact, 80% of coyotes in the wild are under 3 years old. Pup mortality is high, with only 30% - 40% of pups surviving their first year of life. There is a 40% mortality rate for adult coyotes. Most of this mortality is related to humans through activities such as hunting, trapping and poisoning. Transient coyotes have a higher mortality rate than resident coyotes. This makes sense as they are on the move more and more likely to be spotted by humans.

Coyote mortality is high for coyotes of all ages.

Summary

This chapter has provided a condensed synopsis on Eastern coyote biology and ecology. While I've made no attempt to provide all there is to know about all aspects of these areas, the information should be beneficial to coyote hunters. Those folks who internalize this information can apply it to various hunting situations as they occur in the field.

It sometimes takes an array of gear to lure the Eastern coyote into range.

Chapter 2

Coyote Calling Gear

One of the phrases that I share with seminar audiences is that you can kill a coyote by spending as much, or as little, money as you wish. By this I mean that new hunters can use most of their existing deer or turkey gear, obtain a mouth blown distress call, call in, and kill a coyote. In fact, I would advise new coyote hunters to do just that. Give the sport a try without breaking the bank, and see if the sport of coyote calling appeals to you. If, after a few outings, you catch the "calling bug" you can add to your trove of coyote calling gear. This being said, there are a few essential items that will need to start your calling efforts.

Camouflage

There has been some debate as to the overall value of wearing camouflage while coyote hunting. Some schools of thought lessen the benefit of camouflage while others are strong advocates of thoroughly camouflaging your body. I side with the latter group and believe that proper camouflage will give the hunter an advantage. I believe that hunter confidence is important for calling success. If wearing camouflage gives the hunter more confidence, then the hunter will be more successful!

Most experienced coyote hunters agree that motion is the key to alerting approaching coyotes. Hunters who have to ability to sit motionless will stand a better chance of remaining undetected as a coyote comes to the call. By sitting still while wearing properly selected camouflage, the hunter will be putting odds in his favor. With the coyote's keen senses, it is important to meld yourself with your hunting environment. You must attempt to blend in with your surroundings, so be sure to pay attention to this detail. Be sure to wear a face mask and gloves as the head and hands tend to move the most while you call and scan the terrain, waiting for a canine to appear. Also, to break up your human outline, it makes sense to wear different camouflage patterns. For example, wear a jacket of one type of camouflage and pants of another type of camouflage. There are myriads of camouflage patterns on the market today and hunters must rely on their personal preference in deciding which actual pattern to wear.

Northeastern hunters frequently hunt with a blanket of snow covering the terrain. Traditional camouflage patterns will have you sticking out like a sore thumb if you are out in the open. It would be wise decision to obtain white suit, or coverall, to hunt during the winter months. These suits are available at most major hunting retailers. It will help to accessorize in white as well. White colored hat, face mask and gloves will complete your winter snow camouflage.

Here is a tip for hunting in snow camouflage... It is great if you are setting up while actually sitting/lying in the snow. However, if you are set up in brush and the brush does not have snow on it, you will stick out more than if you wear traditional camouflage. If the brush or hedgerow has lots of snow, the white camouflage is just fine. Otherwise, use a traditional gray, brown or green camouflage pattern and nestle among the trees or brush. Another nice tip is to carry a light weight cotton snow camouflage parka in your backpack or vehicle. These articles fit easily over your camouflage and can help you be prepared for any snow condition. They are inexpensive and take away the worry of what to wear as you will always be prepared when you have one at your disposal.

Camouflage at the Next Level:

Wearing camouflage clothing may not be enough while attempting to go unnoticed by the alert eyes of a coyote. It is also good idea to add camouflage to your equipment as well. Rifle barrels and scopes will reflect sunlight and shine like a beacon. I cover mine with cloth camouflage tape, or white sports tape for winter use, for maximum concealment. I use this same tape on my shooting sticks. Paying attention to the small details can mean the difference between success and failure.

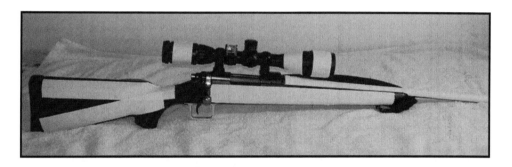

Cloth sports tape makes for cost efficient snow camo for use in winter months.

Decoys

Decoys can be used in conjunction with calling to add realism to the situation. It makes sense to appeal to more than one of the predator's senses and should provide better results for the hunter. When an approaching coyote actually sees a rabbit shaking or bird fluttering, it is more inclined to continue its trek. Coyotes are sight hunters and will approach a call setup more readily if they see something they like. Without a decoy present, coyotes will often stop, or "check-up", to assess the situation. If they check up out of gun range, the hunt may be over.

Decoys serve another important function: They divert attention off the hunter. A decoy and remotely controlled e-call is the perfect combination to attract and hold the attention of an approaching coyote. If the coyote has something to visually focus on, then he may be less aware of the presence of the hunter. This is important if adjustments with your firearm need to be made to take a quality shot.

There are many types/brands of decoys available on the market. It is possible to get remotely controlled, battery operated decoys that feature all the bells and whistles such as sounds, variable motions and lights for night use. Some models are bird decoys that easily clip on to branches and have a revolving wing to attract attention. Great amounts of money need not be spent, however. A feather or piece of fur (real or artificial) hanging from a camouflage aluminum arrow and used it with success.

A wide variety of decoys is available to today's hunter.

I experienced the power of a decoy on a 2009 winter hunt. I was making a morning stand and had a Foxpro Jack-in-the-Box decoy positioned 50 yards away with the FX5 call. After twenty minutes of calling, a coyote came trotting across the field. Despite my best effort, I missed the coyote at a distance of approximately 150 yards. The coyote took off running back in the direction from which it came, so I barked at him to make him stop. Upon hearing my "bark", he turned his head and ran right back into the decoy. This time, I dropped him at 60 yards. I have no doubt that without the decoy; the coyote would have been long gone.

This coyote ran across an open field, in broad daylight, to approach the Jack-in-the-Box decoy.

Firearm Selection

This is really a matter of personal choice and availability. Your decision depends upon the type of terrain you are hunting and the distances you "plan" on shooting. For example, if you are hunting in timber or in areas where visibility provides for a short-range shooting opportunity, a shotgun will fit your needs. Number 4 buckshot is a popular selection. On the other hand, if you are hunting open spaces such as large agricultural fields or open range, a center fire rifle may serve you better. Popular choices here are .223 and .22-250. The .204 caliber has become popular in recent years and it is an excellent choice for killing coyotes.

The increase in pelt value in recent years has caused many hunters to be concerned with their firearm choice. Providing minimal damage is an issue that causes many hunters to use smaller calibers such as the .22 magnum and the .17 hmr. These calibers are also "neighborhood friendly" when hunting near suburban areas, yet will still take down eastern coyotes. Hunters who favor these calibers typically like to keep the shot distances well inside of 100 yards.

Coyote Rounds: .22mag, .204, .223 and 10 gauge.

A 55-grain ballistic tip was not friendly to this fur.

Shooting Accessories

Let's define shooting accessories as items brought afield to make your shooting more dependable. At the moment of truth, when the adrenaline is flowing, and muscles are shaking at the sight of an approaching coyote, the hunter needs to be able to complete the hunt with a quality shot. Nothing will make the shot steadier than a solid rest. There are many styles/brands of bi-pods and shooting sticks to choose from. The Harris bipod is a solid performer. The only drawback with it is that the legs are not long enough to be used comfortably while the hunter is sitting on a stool or chair. If the hunter is using only a pad, or chooses to sit on the bare ground, the Harris bipod is hard to beat. Primos and Bog-Pod make terrific telescopic monopods, bi-pods and tri-pods than will work wonderfully, no matter what the hunter uses to sit upon. Their products are easily, and quietly, adjustable to accommodate any desired height requirements.

When hunting in snowy conditions, it is not comfortable to sit in the snow over periods of time. For this reason, the use a folding chair to get off the wet ground is recommended. Some folding chairs actually double as a backpack with storage that allows items such as decoys and lights/batteries for night hunts to be carried with ease. Many hunters like to carry binoculars while they hunt. I used to carry binoculars with me each time I ventured out. I have gotten away from this practice lately because I found that I could catch the coyote's motion with my peripheral vision quicker when I wasn't spending time glassing. When hunting areas that have large fields, I will sometimes still carry binoculars with me.

One piece of optics that is truly valuable is a rangefinder. They need not be carried on every hunt, though. When visiting a location for the first time, use the rangefinder on various landmarks to get an idea of distances for incoming coyotes. It's also nice to have the rangefinder present to verify distances of critters you've shot or missed. These days there are many models on the market. The Bushnell Scout is recommended because it is compact and lightweight.

Accessories, such as these, will allow for more effective shooting.

At the Next Level: All-Purpose Shooting Sticks

I have given my bipod a makeover that has increased its effectiveness in the field. These modifications can be done to any shooting stick or incorporated when building a pair of homemade sticks. The cost of the modification is minimal. Most commercially produced shooting sticks are black in color. As an advocate for maximum camouflage, I felt it best to dress up my bipod to match the surrounding of where I hunt. Painting the bipod white was truly not effective because half the time I was hunting in snow-free conditions. The solution was simple. White cloth sports tape was applied in a single strip down one side of each pole. On the other side of the pole, camouflage cloth tape was applied. The result is a bipod that is ready for all season use! In snowy conditions, simply face the white side of the sticks outwards. When no snow is present, simply face the camouflage side outwards. This cost-effective procedure takes away the need to purchase two separate shooting sticks.

The author's shooting sticks are modified to include custom camo and a mouse squeaker call attached for convenient use!

 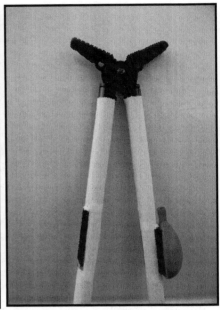

Shooting sticks can be dressed with cloth tape for camo in any season.

One of the greatest modifications to any shooting stick is the addition of a squeaker type call. Be sure to place the squeaker (I prefer an oval shaped bulb squeaker) at a comfortable height on the shooting stick. The motion of your hand trying to operate the call may be detected by incoming predators. I have found that it is best to position the squeaker near the top of the stick so that it is convenient to operate as you brace for a shot. To maximize versatility, attach the call with Velcro. Furthermore, place a strip of Velcro on each pole. This is vital because the bulb squeaker can be switched from side to side depending upon on which camouflage is facing outward. If the call is placed on one pole only, the hunter will have an inconvenient reach for the call. There was a time, in my field trials, when I applied a call on each pole. However, that led to too many errant squeaks by hitting the call by mistake. The use of Velcro has proved to be more efficient.

Types of Calls

There are a wide variety of calls available to today's predator hunter. From production mouth calls to high tech digital calls that feature hundreds of pre-recorded sounds, there is a call to fit every hunter's budget. Let's take a look at what is offered to hunters today...

Hand Calls

Hand-held rabbit distress calls, also called mouth calls, have probably accounted for more dead coyotes than all other calls combined. Hand calls are categorized as either closed reed or open reed. Furthermore, they are made to produce either distress sounds or to mimic sounds of coyotes. Let's look at each type of call separately...

<u>Closed Reed Calls</u>: The main characteristic of this type of call is that the "voice"- the part of the call that produces sound when air is forced through it-is located inside the body, or barrel, of the call. These calls are easy to learn and use and are recommended for first time callers. By cupping a hand over the end of the barrel, the sound can be muffled and the tone can be altered. Closed reed calls have two common drawbacks. One is that they generally produce only one type of sound per call, which limits their versatility. There are a few calls on the market that allow the hunter to rotate a barrel on the call that allows for 2 or 3 sounds to be produced. Secondly, closed reed calls tend to "Freeze" when used in colder temperatures. This occurs when saliva from the hunter comes in contact with the internal reed and freezes. The call sound is hampered dramatically when this occurs and hunter frustration is soon to follow. Some hunters attempt to remedy this occurrence by storing the call in an internal pocket while not calling. It has been my experience, however, that a call that tends to "freeze-up" will do so at the most inopportune time.

Closed reed calls are easy and comfortable to operate.

Open Reed Calls: With this type of call, the "voice", or reed, is exposed. The hunter is to gently bite down, with teeth or lips, on the reed, and then blow air, to produce the desired sound. Like closed reed calls, there are pros and cons associated with open reed calls. First off, since the reed to exposed, these calls are more resilient to freezing-up. This simply means that they are more reliable in terms of being able to perform for the entire duration of the stand. Also, open reed calls have the ability to produce a wide range of sounds. By placing teeth or lips at different positions on the reed, the pitch of the call is altered. When using an open reed rabbit distress call, it is quite possible to authentically re-produce the sounds of birds, raccoons, rodents, etc. A common drawback to using open reed calls is that they take more practice time to master. Additionally, for some folks they are not as comfortable to use as closed reed calls, as the reed can vibrate in the mouth.

Open reed calls allow hunters to produce variable sounds from each call.

The Mouse Squeaker Call

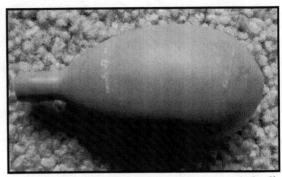

Another type of air blown predator call that warrants discussion is the squeaker type call. In my opinion, this type of call is greatly underappreciated in its ability to call in coyotes. Squeakers can be a mouth blown or a bulb type call that needs to be squeezed to operate. A bulb squeaker attached to a shooting stick or fore-end of a rifle is a deadly call. Squeakers are excellent coaxers that can be used to lure in coyotes that "check up" during their approach.

Hand calls, either closed or open reed or prey distress or coyote howlers, are available through chain sporting goods stores or through retailers on the internet. Almost all major hunting call companies have jumped on the predator call bandwagon and have added predator calls to their product line.

Another facet of the hand call business that has grown in popularity is the custom call market. These calls, which are often works of art to behold, can produce ultra-realistic sounds. Perhaps the best source for locating custom calls is to search on popular internet forums such as the Predator Masters website.

Ultimately, it is up to the hunter to experiment with and choose which type of call they prefer. It is a good idea to have an assortment of calls available to address your hunting needs.

No matter what type of hand call you use, it is a good idea to keep your calls on a lanyard while hunting. These around-your-neck ropes, will keep your calls secure, organized and ready to reach when you need them. The last thing you want to do is fumble around searching for your call when a critter is near. Worse yet is to drop a $ 65.00 custom call in 8 inches of snow in the dark. Like calls, all lanyards are not created equally. Hunters can choose production models from major call manufacturers or a custom version. Most serious hunters use a custom version as they are less likely to allow calls to become entangled.

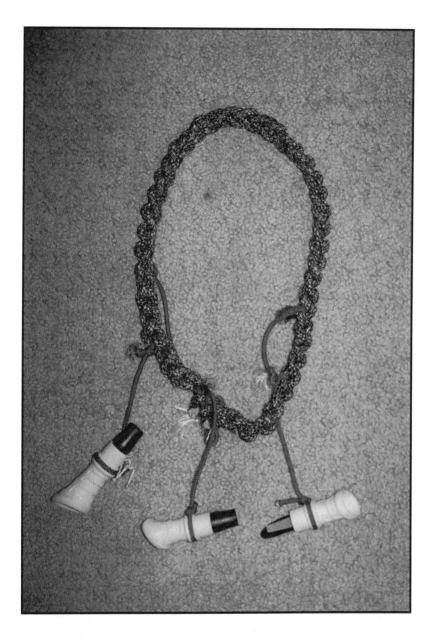

It is a good idea to keep a variety of hand calls on your lanyard so that you have options in every scenario.

At the Next Level: The History of Predator Calls

For the hand call enthusiast, collecting an assortment of hand calls in inevitable. For many predator callers, collecting such calls is a hobby. From vintage models to the latest designs, it is interesting to observe the progression of predator calls. A terrific source to research the evolution of mouth calls is "Predator Calls, The First 50 Years" by Jay Nistetter. This 300-page book is filled with information and pictures of the rarest and most unique calls ever produced. Simply said, it is a must for the predator call enthusiast.

Jay Nistetter's book is considered a "must read" for the call enthusiast. (Photo courtesy of Abner J. Druckenmiller)

Call collectors should consider a trip to the Predator Call Museum which is located at the Foxpro facility in Lewistown, PA. Steve Dillon has acquired an awe-inspiring collection of early electronic and mouth blown calls. The museum also features artifacts, such as belt buckles, patches and shirts, from various predator clubs as well as calling contests from around the country. The walls are adorned with numerous framed photographs featuring pioneers of the predator calling community.

The Predator Call Museum at the Foxpro facility offers a glimpse at calling history.

Electronic calls

Electronic calls have become increasingly popular over the years and companies continue to evolve their product line. All electronic calls, sometimes known as e-callers, will call in predators and all have their strong points and weak points. When deciding upon which e-caller to purchase, the buyer must be aware of certain features and variables in electronic callers....

- Weight of the unit
- Presence/length of wires
- Loudness of projected sound
- Clarity of sound
- Number of sounds unit can store/play
- Type of battery/ battery life
- Bulk and ease of use
- Remote control capabilities
- Cost of unit and additional sounds

There is a long list of benefits to using electronic callers. First off, they offer clear, realistic sounds. Users of mouth calls sometimes wonder if the sounds they are trying to emit are adequate to call in a coyote. In other words, "Do they sound good enough?" By using an electronic call, all doubt can be removed. Most of the sounds in today's e-callers are recordings of actual live animals. Additionally, there are literally hundreds of sounds available to choose from when using e-callers. Some upper end models store and play 500 sounds. This may seem extreme, but it is always nice to have the option of selecting a unique sound in certain situations.

Electronic callers are easy to use and let the hunter concentrate on other aspects of the hunt. For hunters who do not wish to blow into a mouth call, or for those who may have health issues, and can't blow for extended periods of time, e-callers are the way to go. Units that have the ability to be operated through a remote control have a huge advantage in that they help hunters stage how a coyote will approach a setup. This will be covered in great detail in upcoming chapters.

Despite the positive attributes of e-callers, it is not a given that a hunter will kill a coyote every time he uses one. That's just the way it goes in predator calling. The effective use of e-callers goes beyond plunking one down in the field, turning it on, and waiting for a predator to approach. There are certain things to know about their use that can increase hunter satisfaction. I have compiled a list of tips to enhance the effectiveness and enjoyment of electronic calls.

<u>Battery Freshness</u>   For optimal performance of your call, make sure that the batteries are at full strength. Many units now use rechargeable NiMH batteries. Re-charge your batteries after each calling venture. If you call has not been used in a while, give the batteries a charge before you head afield. NiMH batteries lose 1% of their charge each day, so you want to be sure that the batteries have a full charge. If your call uses a remote control, be sure that the battery in the remote is also fresh. It will be good idea to carry extra batteries in a pocket for long days or nights of hunting. There is never a good time to have battery failure, and a hunt can be saved if batteries can be changed in the field.

<u>Volume selection</u>   Many hunters question just how loud they should be playing their e-callers. A safe bet is to start at a lower volume and increase volume as they stand progresses. The idea of starting with a softer volume is that any close proximity predators will not spook at the low volume sound as the sound first plays. Many hunters will set the volume of the main call at ½ to ¾ of full volume. The terrain and weather often dictates volume levels. In wide open spaces or in windy conditions, use more volume.

<u>Elevation</u>   Believe it or not, raising the call just a few feet above the ground will maximize both sound quality and operation performance. When calls are placed directly on the ground, the sound can be muffled by grass, snow, undergrowth, etc. When possible, place the call on an elevated feature to maximize the sound carrying ability. A fencepost, tree stump or limb can work wonderfully. Additionally, remote controlled calls operate much more efficiently when the call is elevated and there is no interference between the call and the remote. When I set up in a field

in the winter, I bring along a white 5-gallon plastic bucket. I place the call on the bucket and the call is sufficiently raised for optimum performance. Additionally, the white coloration provides an instant camouflage

Remote placement distance   Another frequently heard question is… "How far away should I place the call from my setup position?" Remember, predators will likely circle the sound source from the downwind position. The key is to place the unit so that they circle the call and give the hunter a quality shot opportunity. The answer to our question lies in the hunter's hunting style. If using a shot gun, the distance between hunter and call should be 20-35 yards. Rifle hunters will benefit from placing the call out at a distance of 50-80 yards.

Sound Selection A common question from new e-call owners is… "What sounds should I put on my call?" It stands to good reason to include a variety of distress sounds of animals that are on the coyote's diet. Various rodent, rabbit and bird sounds will be effective. Hunters who are not confident in using mouth howlers, but wish to get into using coyote vocalizations, will love the realistic howls that the e-calls provide.

I have used several brands of e-callers throughout the years and have decided that, when using the criteria mentioned prior, that the calls made by Foxpro Game Calls fit my needs most directly. Add superior customer service and a company that does more for the predator hunting community than any other, and you have a winning combination.

Foxpro's Fury (left) and FX3 allow hunters to opportunity to use state of the art digitally recorded sound.

At the Next Level: Beacon for calls

Setting your electronic call on the ground during night hunts can result in a frustrating and embarrassing result... Losing the call! If the call can't be seen as it sits camouflaged in the darkness, the hunter could have a lengthy search ahead. The best way to find the call is to play a sound and simply follow the sound. No problem, or shame, in doing that. However, if the batteries are dead or the unit is not on for some reason, the search is on! I've done this and have heard the snickering of my partner in the darkness. I soon wised up and placed a strip of reflective tape on the call. By doing so, the call can easily be found by shining your spot light, and your time will be better spent hunting instead of searching in the darkness for your misplaced call. Try using reflective white tape when using white or LED light as the red tape does not reflect very well.

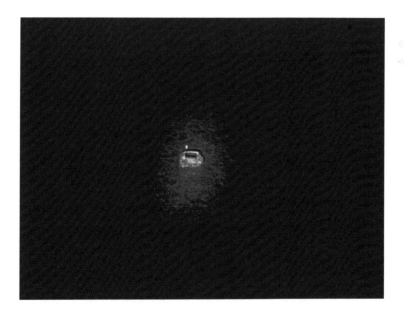

A strip of reflective tape on your call will allow you to find it in the dark.

Building healthy relationships with landowners will result in years of hunting enjoyment.

Chapter 3

Obtaining Permission

One of the keys of success for effective coyote hunting is to have a large amount of hunting land available. Additionally, it is important not to call an area too often. If you only have a handful of farms to hunt, you will surely overcall them during the course of a season. The predators will get used to the hunting pressure quickly and calling success will drop dramatically. Hence, having numerous farms or land access will help alleviate this problem. Furthermore, choosing hunting spots should depend upon wind direction. Some locations will be more favorable in certain wind directions, for both the approach and the actual hunting. Certain farms may have to be skipped altogether due to wind direction. For these reasons, it is important to have as many hunting spots as possible.

It is getting more and more difficult to find areas to hunt these days. Urban and suburban folk who are buying farmlands are simply not in tune with hunting as a way of life. For this reason, they are reluctant to grant permission to access their land for the purpose of hunting. Luckily for the coyote hunter, few landowners want coyotes around. As a result,

it is easier to obtain permission for hunting them than for hunting deer or turkey. By following the information presented in this chapter, you will be more successful in obtaining land to hunt.

Predators do not know who owns land. State lands hold coyotes and should not be overlooked. The secret to hunting them is to be one of the first callers of the season in the area. Get the jump on the competition by calling these parcels early in the season. If you favor a public access land but others are hunting it, go there during late night hours when other hunters may be home fast asleep in their warm beds.

Actually, there is good news and bad news regarding accessing private lands for predator hunting. The good news is that many landowners do not want the coyotes around. The bad news is that the act of seeking permission takes work and let's face it... some nerve. Hunting private land is like dancing with the most beautiful girl in the bar, you won't be doing either, unless you ask! I break down this act of permission seeking into two categories. One is the "casual inquiry." You are at a party or an event and the topic of land comes up and someone mentions coyotes chasing deer or the loss of a pet. You seize the easy opportunity and mention that you call predators and would love come out to their property.

The other type of permission seeking is the dreaded "door knock". This occurs when you see a likely looking farm or territory as you drive around and you stop by the house to seek permission. This is where your nerve comes into play. Will you be well received? Or, will you be interrupting the occupants? There are some things you can do to make the permission seeking procedure more comfortable for both parties.

When asking permission, do so at a convenient time for the landowner. Try not to interrupt them during lunch or dinner. If possible, try to arrive when the landowner is already outside. It is an automatic invasion of privacy if you have to interrupt them from indoor activities. Whenever possible, seek permission far in advance of the hunting season. This shows the landowner that you are organized in your efforts. From your perspective, you may beat out other hunters who wish to gain permission to hunt there as well. When first pulling up in your vehicle to seek permission, do so slowly and don't slam vehicle doors. A nice, calm approach can affect the landowners' attitude right away. It is a good idea to wear conservative clothing when seeking permission. Wearing camouflage is not recommended. In talking to landowners, be courteous at all times, even in rejection. Remember that it is their right to grant or deny permission.

If all goes well and you are granted permission, you may want to clarify a few issues. First off, ask where is best place to park your vehicle?

You surely don't want your truck to be in the way of any farming activities. Ask if you can hunt the property during night time hours. This is sometimes a foreign idea to many folks, so establish permission for night hunting right away. Ask the landowner if they have any specific rules regarding your hunting their property and be sure to follow them. Finally, ask if they have any dogs as pets, and see if the pets are normally tied up, or kept inside, at night while you may be there hunting.

Once permission has been granted, it is important to stay in good graces with the landowner. After the season, it would be a nice gesture to return with a gift of appreciation. Find out what the person likes to eat or drink or even what their hobbies are. At holiday time, a note or card with a gift certificate to a local restaurant is always appreciated. By being a good sportsman and respecting the land and the landowner's wishes, you can ensure a positive hunting experience for future years. If you treat them right, you will be welcomed back.

On the other hand, certain behaviors will certainly put future hunts at risk. Never drive in a farmer's field without permission. Along these lines, do not drive across a field or even a laneway when it is wet or muddy. Don't bring additional guests without permission. Landowners may feel as if they know how you act while hunting, but they may be unsure about additional hunters on their land. Do not assume that you have permission to hunt other species after coyote season ends. By doing so, you will be viewed as taking advantage of the situation and that is not a good thing. Last, but not least, clean up after yourself. Do not leave empty brass or candy wrappers behind. Littering is the ultimate sign of disrespect.

You will be all smiles when you maintain healty relationships with landowners.

At the Next Level: The Coyote Hunter's Business Card

It is a good idea to present a coyote hunting "business" card to landowners. On the card, include your contact information, such as phone number and address. By offering this information, you are showing the landowner that you can be trustworthy and available if any concerns arise. I've even had landowners share the contact information and picked up additional farms to hunt as a result. Your coyote hunting "business" card can be thought of as an inexpensive way to advertise.

Business cards are relatively inexpensive to get printed online. They can also be designed on a home computer and printed at home. Images to include on your card can be found on various clip art websites. Have fun in designing your card and remember it will be a reflection of you, so choose pictures and phrasing carefully.

Realistic shooting practice will result in better results during the season.

Chapter 4

Perfect Practice

Nothing is more frustrating than calling in a coyote and missing when shooting. Now, don't get me wrong, everybody misses from time to time. However, if a hunter realizes that his killing percentage is way too low, it may be time to take action. By action, I mean engaging in proper practice techniques. The old adage "Practice makes perfect" is not actually true. In reality, it should read... "Perfect practice makes perfect." If practicing shooting with a coyote rifle does not accurately simulate an actual hunting situation, then the perfect practice is not happening. I have developed two distinct practice scenarios that are perfect for coyote hunters. One of the techniques deals with increasing accuracy while shooting in complete darkness of night. The second technique assists in making tough daytime shots. Both of these techniques will take your shooting abilities to the next level!

Red Eye Targets

There is good news and bad news for hunters who are able to call for coyotes at night. The good news is that hunters can expect action packed hunts with good likelihood that they will get coyotes to respond. The bad news is that making a successful killing shot is much more difficult at night than it is in daylight. Early in my calling career, I experienced a dry spell when many coyotes were called in, but missed at the moment of truth! Dwelling on my lack of shooting prowess, I came up with a plan... I needed practice, and not just any shooting practice. I needed to develop a night hunting shooting situation so that my success rate would increase.

The idea was to invent a practice scenario that would replicate an actual night hunting session. In order to accomplish this, targets needed to be created that would resemble a predator at night. After some initial brainstorming and trial and error target tinkering, I choose to use staked driveway reflectors. The

stakes are nice because they are easy to carry and can stick into most dirt surfaces. To make the reflectors resemble the glowing eyes of a coyote, I placed two pennies on each reflector and painted the reflector black. When the coins were removed, the reflective portion highly resembled "eyes" when lit up with a red-lens sport light and viewed through a rifle scope.

The reflective targets can be set up at known distances and shot

using the same gear that would be used during an actual hunt. Remember, the goal here is to simulate an actual night time hunt. Using the same rifle, bipod and chair or cushion is part of the procedure. Shooting at these types of targets is as close to real thing as you are going to get. It is amazing how the glowing "eyes" of the reflectors look like the real thing as they are viewed through the rifle scope. Practice holding the reticule between the eyes when you take the shot. Analysis of the reflectors will provide feedback as to where your bullets hit in the dark.

Because few rifle ranges are open for night time shooting, this type of practice will most likely take place on private land. Be sure to communicate your intentions with the landowner before engaging in your practice sessions. After I began using this night time practice technique, my shooting success rate soared.

Meet Rover!

The next phase of my shooting practice called for the development of a practice scenario that would replicate an actual daytime coyote hunt. I went to the drawing board and came up with "Rover," a motorized coyote target that allows for practicing multiple shots at various distances

Rover was originally a remotely controlled monster truck that was purchased at Radio Shack. The vehicle needed to go through a transformation before it would be ready for its new purpose. After removing the plastic shell of a monster truck, the flat chassis was revealed.

The remotely driven "Rover" target provides realistic shooting practice at random distances.

53

I mounted a life size coyote paper target to the chassis. This was accomplished by gluing an archery target to a like size piece of cardboard. A can of aerosol spray glue was perfect for the job. The cardboard provided a sturdy backing for the target to ensure that the coyote would always be visible to the shooter. The low center of gravity of the chassis allows the target to remain upright while the target is moving across surfaces such as cut fields or gravel pits.

Although practicing with Rover can be done successfully by a solo shooter, the practice is best executed when a partner is present Partners can take turns at shooting and at driving Rover around the field or gravel pit For safety sake, pay close attention to all areas to ensure that a backstop is present no matter where the moving target may be located. To maximize realism, the shooter should use the exact same equipment that they would during an actual hunt. If you use a shooting aid such as shooting sticks or a bi-pod, by all means, use them in this practice session.

Furthermore, position yourself as you would during a calling sequence as opposed to shooting off a bench and rest. Remember, this practice plan is attempting to re-create all the elements of an actual hunt. Shooting position is an integral part of a hunter's setup.

One person "drives" Rover while the shooter attempts to keep him in the scope.

Although practicing with a target such as Rover sounds like all fun and games, there are some noteworthy benefits associated with it. First off, this type of practice lends itself perfectly to being able to better judge distances in the field. Many times, practice shots are taken at a range using stationary targets set at known distances of 50, 100 and 150 yards. By tradition, shooters start out by shooting the close targets and then set the target progressively farther away. This is standard technique for sighting in rifles and many hunters consider this shooting time their "practice". By using Rover's random distance scenario, the shot distances are variable and this helps shooters become proficient at judging distances in the field. By taking repeated shots at targets at unknown distances in a field situation and making educated attempts to determine the distances, hunters can become more consistent in judging distances and hitting targets. Initially, shooters may want to confirm their field judging with a rangefinder to confirm distances. This will provide quick feedback to the shooter's ability to estimate distance.

This type of practice is also perfect for allowing hunters the opportunity to increase familiarity with their rifles. What better way to gain a feel for a rifle than by using it in a situation that replicates an actual hunt so vividly? It will let hunters know exactly how their rifles will perform at a wide range of distances in the field. Knowing just where your rifle will hit at distances between 100 and 200 yards, will boost confidence while afield. Furthermore, it will give a good indication of a hunter's skill level at shooting at different distances. If targets are frequently missed at a certain distance, the shooter can concentrate on improving their accuracy at that given distance. Knowledge of individual shooting ability will make anyone a better shooter and hunter.

Rover also provides an excellent opportunity to increase skill at hitting a moving target. We would all like coyotes to stand still and give us a broadside shot. However, that is not always the case. It has been said that the best time to shoot a coyote is at the first opportunity. If a coyote is trotting in, and attempting to wind a hunter, the hunter had better shoot before the coyote reaches the hunters scent cone. In this case, the necessary shot is often a moving shot and that is seldom easy accomplished. By having your partner continuously move Rover about the field, realistic practice for the dreaded moving shot can occur.

Learning where to hold on a moving target and becoming accustomed to taking moving shots will transfer nicely when it comes time to shot at a real coyote as it races into a calling setup.

Perfect practice may lead to great moments afield!

A third benefit to using Rover is that actual hunting situations can be duplicated. For example, hunters have long used to technique of "barking" to a running coyote to make it stop for a more manageable shot. This technique can be easily practiced when you have a partner present. Imagine tracking Rover in your scope as it zips across the field. When you feel that Rover is positioned at an appropriate distance make a "bark" or "woof" with your mouth. Upon hearing this, your partner should stop Rover. Now, you must settle your sights on the target and take your best shot. The mental and physical adjustment from watching a running coyote in your scope to watching it stop broadside, and squeezing the trigger, can be the difference in a kill or another educated coyote. Practice that replicates this adjustment will pay off.

Serious predator hunters are believers in being well prepared. A large portion of preparation should be devoted to improving marksmanship skills. It stands to reason that the best way to become a better shooter is to shoot more often. By using specialized targets, such as the Night Eyes Reflectors and Rover, hunters can easily engage in realistic shooting practice. It is practice that is exciting, beneficial and will result in more dead coyotes during the season!

Proper setup is just factor to come into play while trying to achieve success while calling to Eastern coyotes.

Chapter 5

Factors of Successful Hunting

To be consistently successful, the hunter must pay attention, in great detail, to the many variables and factors that come into play while calling coyotes. Surely, there is more to the sport than just getting afield and blowing into a call. In this chapter, we examine the many factors that affect calling success. I'd like to point out that the act of calling is a factor, in itself, and shall be discussed in Chapter 6. Our discussion here will include hunting techniques and strategies such as proper scouting, safety practices, approach, setup and shooting. When we add variables such as weather factors, hunting pressure and coyote density and the whole realm of predator calling can seem complex.

Scouting

Scouting can be described as analyzing an area for the presence of a desired game species. There are many ways to scout for predator hunting success. The first is the traditional method of inspecting land for obvious sign that predators have been in the area. Fresh tracks in snow or mud, scat, den sites, and witnessing predators are all examples of this type of scouting. The key word here is *fresh*. Old tracks in mud or old scat are just that... old news. Be on the lookout for fresh sign that indicates that the coyotes are presently using the area. Extra fresh tracks in snow can actually be followed and will lead right up to a bedded or foraging coyote.

Another form of scouting involves the use of trail cameras. Trail cameras should not be thought of as a "deer-only" hunting aid. By placing a camera near well used travel routes it is possible to find out exactly when the coyotes are using the area. Cameras that have the ability to record the exact time that coyotes are passing through are truly beneficial. If a pattern is established, a hunter will know exactly when he needs to be hunting a certain farm. Trail cameras are effective because they can work around the clock for you.

Audible scouting is a bona fide method to locating packs. Since coyotes are prone to respond to howling, ether real or manmade, the hunter can use this to his advantage. In the weeks prior to the calling season, try to find packs to hunt by getting them to sound off to your howling. By using a mouth howler, or by playing howls with an e-caller, the hunter can locate coyotes to hunt. It is interesting to note that pre-recorded siren sounds are highly effective at triggering a response from resident coyotes. Whatever sound you choose, the technique requires driving around at dusk or early dawn, howling and listening for real coyotes to howl back. If they do respond, and it is in an area where you normally hunt, it's a safe bet that they will be around during hunting season. If the howling is coming from an area where you do not have permission, now is the time to sweet talk the landowner and try to get access. One thing is likely; the more hunting locations that you can get that hold coyotes on a regular basis, the more success you should have while calling there.

There is another type of coyote scouting that relies upon listening. This time, however, you are not listening to coyotes, but to landowners.

Through regular contact with landowners, they can provide feedback as to when and where they are seeing and hearing coyotes. Let's face it... the landowner spends more time at their farms than anyone else. They should be most aware of what is happening on their acreage. If a farmer is nice enough to share his sightings with you, take advantage and follow their heed. If successful in the quest, show or tell the landowner about the outcome and they will be inclined to share more information with you in the future.

Yet another type of scouting is actually a hunting technique and/or strategy. It is very similar to "Run & Gun" or "Cut & Run" turkey hunting and can be thought of as "immediate needs" scouting. In this scenario, the hunter drives around the area and howls at select locations with hope of getting a response back. If the coyotes respond, the hunter goes ahead, sets up and calls. If no response is heard, the hunter moves along to the next area tries again. It is beneficial to a large amount of land permission to use this technique

Safety Issues

No matter what type of hunting sportsman are engaged in, there is underlying aspect of safety conduct and issues that must be addressed. Coyote callers are no exception and must take special care to insure safe outings... every time out!

Any hunter who goes through a hunter's education course is taught the basic rules for firearms safety. As a refresher, these are...

1.) Keep your barrel pointed in a safe direction at all times
2.) Keep your finger off the trigger until you are ready to shoot
3.) Keep all guns unloaded until you are ready to use them

While these rules are hugely important, coyote callers should utilize some very specific guidelines to insure maximum safety. These steps, and correlating techniques, take safety awareness to the next level.

Step 1: Get to know your partner

    Although I hunt alone a great majority of the time, hunting with a partner is often fun and rewarding. It also calls for enhanced awareness of safety concerns. I learned this the hard way. Luckily, I'm here to write about it. An acquaintance from work wanted to hook up for an afternoon/early night hunt. I picked him up at his house, and we were off for short drive to a farm that was new to the both of us. It was still light when we set up. I placed our stools next to each other, and walked out to place the e-call. Suddenly, I heard the "Crack" of a .223! I spun around and there is my new partner looking confused as he stared at his rifle. Fortunately, his muzzle wasn't pointed at me. After an empty set, we moved to another section of the farm and wouldn't you know it… the same thing happened again! I requested that he not use the rifle again and learned a lesson myself: when hunting with someone for the first time, stay in close proximity to them so that you can share your insight with them and to ensure that no safety blunders occur. Once you get to know a person, then you can take on more varied setup options.

Step 2: Always know where your hunting partner is located

Develop a light signal so you always know the location of your partner.

    It is imperative to know exactly where each person is located. For safeties sake, it may be best to simply sit side by side. It's easy to whisper to each other and fun to share the hunt. For some locations, however, the practice of "splitting up to cover the terrain" is beneficial. When separating during a hunt, day or night, it is vital to know your partner's location. This fact takes on new significance when calling in the dark. It may be necessary to physically walk a partner to your setup location and show him where you will be sitting. Once set up, during night hunts, it is important to re-confirm locations. Develop a signal like blinking your spotlights towards each other.

Once in position, and the calling has started, it is best not to move to a different location. The temptation to move to gain a better view of landscape occurs frequently. When hunting solo, re-locating is no big deal. However, when a partner is involved, moving may be a costly mistake. If you *have* to move for any reason, use a 2-way radio or cell phone to communicate your intentions. If no verbal communication is possible, stay put for the entire stand. Remember, it is vital to know your hunting partner's exact location.

Step 3: Safe Scanning Techniques

When scanning for coyotes, be sure to do so with a hand-held spotlight instead of a light affixed to a firearm. A safety issue immediately occurs when hunters point their guns in random directions, especially in the darkness.

Scanning with a gun-mounted light is not the best practice!

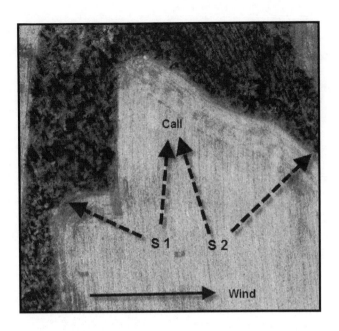

Pre-plan scanning & shooting areas when hunting with a partner.

Step 4: The "Hunt's Over" Signal

At the end of a calling set, it may be necessary to establish a signal to say "The hunt's over". On the occasions when partners are not within whispering distance, a specific sound should be played. Again, this must be communicated between partners prior to the hunt. I advise using a specific stand ending sound that is hard to misinterpret. During night hunts, I play crow fight sounds on my Foxpro call. During day hunts, I play elk bugle sounds (keep in mind, I live in New York). Once these sounds are played, it is clear that the hunt is over, no shooting is allowed, and it is time to gather and carry on.

It is important to not let emotions of the hunt take over. Keep a cool head and think before you shoot. Although no one plans on having an accident, we can plan to reduce its likelihood. Hunters may wish to re-examine their own hunting techniques and consider the safety steps discussed here.

When to Call/Hunt

For weekend hunters who are seeking the optimum time slot to hunt, it would seem obvious that the best time to call to a predator is when the predator is naturally roaming and looking for food. As discussed in Chapter 1, coyotes travel most frequently between 6 PM and 6AM. Furthermore, the greatest distances are traveled during the morning hours. Hence, it would be advantageous to hunt at dusk and dawn (and certainly at night where permissible by law). Many hunters report that they like to wait until midnight and beyond to call for coyotes, citing that they like to let the environment settle down before the attempt to call. My personal log books, however, show no distinct time of darkness that is superior to any other. My ultimate determining factor of when to hunt relies far more on weather conditions than time of night. These factors will be discussed in the weather section of this chapter.

Although night time may be the right time for calling coyotes, successful calling can occur at mid-day. Contest hunters, who do not wish to waste a minute of calling opportunity, should make attempts to call in day-time coyotes. Despite the fact that mid-day is generally a time of rest and seclusion for Eastern coyotes, they can and will respond to calling. This is especially true when the weather is cold and coyotes, driven by hunger, will be on the prowl for sustaining food. The adage "You can't get them sitting on the couch," certainly applies to daytime coyote calling.

Approach

Many hunts may actually end before they start with a sloppy approach to the calling setup. Lack of attention to small details can result in big failure. Keep in mind that your hunt actually starts before you ever get out of your car. A stealthy arrival should be part of your plan. For starters, make sure your vehicle is quiet. A loud muffler may startle wary coyotes. I once had a new set of brakes installed on my Jeep. As luck would have it, each time I applied the brakes, a piercing squeak could be heard. I'm sure I alerted more than one coyote before I took the Jeep back to the shop. Once you have arrived at your destination, care should be taken regarding your vehicle. For example, be careful in parking your vehicle too close to your setup. Hide your car from the vision of the predators. Park behind a hill, and plan to call from the other side of it. This is especially true for daytime hunts. On several occasions, at night, I've seen coyotes run right past my parked truck. Be aware of any noises that your car will make once stopped. Some vehicles will make bell sounds when doors are opened and keys are still in the ignition, for example. Of course, do not slam the doors as you exit the vehicle.

Attempt to park your vehicle so that it is inconspicuous.

When walking to a setup location, be as quiet as possible. Be aware of crossing fences and walking over any structures that create unnatural noise. Additionally, make sure that your equipment is not banging or bouncing around, making noise with each step you take. For example, keep calls and remote controls inside your clothing so that they do not swing and make noise.

Make sure that your scent is not blowing into the area as you approach.

You may read elsewhere to discuss any relevant plans with your partner while you are inside the car and not talk as you walk to the setup. I believe that this is a little extreme. Whispering on route is OK by me. Although I hunt alone 90% of the time, the whole aspect of camaraderie is lost if you limit yourself to talking only before and after a hunt. Use common sense with your partner, and you should have no detrimental effect on your approach.

Sound is not the only issue when talking about a proper approach. Odor control must also be considered. If a coyote detects your scent, he will most likely vacate the area before you even know he was there. To deter this from happening, there are a couple of things you need to be aware of. First, it would be best not to walk through any area when you anticipate a predator to approach your calling. By doing so, an approaching coyote may cross your footpath. They will catch the "hot scent" and go on instant alert. Typically, this means they will double back in the direction they came as they know it is safe. Lesson learned? The scent you lay down is as important as the scent the wind will carry. Speaking of wind, while approaching your stand, do so with the wind in your face. If it is at your back, you will be broadcasting your presence before the hunt starts. Again, this will be detrimental to success. Minimizing unnatural sounds and smells as you approach is paramount to calling success.

When approaching a setup, hunters also need to honor the coyote's keen sense of sight. Coyotes can pick up on even the slightest motion, far or near, so use extreme caution while walking. Move through available landscape features to hide you as you approach. Walk along hedgerows instead of cutting across open fields. Be sure not to expose yourself be walking on a skyline such as a ridge or hill top. If hunters pay attention to these details, the scales will be tipped in their favor.

The importance of proper setup should never be underestimated!

Proper Setup

Of all the factors presented in this book, proper setup is the most important. You could make mistakes in perhaps each of the other factors, and still have some sort of success. However, setting up improperly will result in empty stands, blown shot opportunities and educated coyotes. Setups may change in respect to terrain features, but the underlying principles remain the same. Hunters need to allow the coyote to feel secure in approaching and allow themselves an opportunity to take a quality shot. Probably the most important issue concerning proper setup is to use the wind in your favor. There has been some debate about how to do this. Although there are few absolutes in coyote calling, coyotes will very often attempt to circle into a downwind position of the call source. Why do they do this? It is their attempt to survey the scene and make sure it is safe to approach. Their astute noise will tell them who is the culprit involved at the "death scene."

The common question is… Should you set up with the wind blowing in your face or with the wind blowing at your back? If you analyze the situation, both scenarios could make sense. Let's make a virtual setup…you are on the top of a cut hayfield. At the bottom edge of the field is a wooded area that you believe is holding coyotes. Hedge rows border the field to your right and to your left. You are nestled against a hay bale and have a panoramic view of the entire field. In this fictional dusk or dawn daylight hunt, you are using a mouth blown rabbit call and carry a .223 Remington.

If the wind is blowing into your face, you are anticipating that the approaching coyotes will leave the woods and come along a hedge row or up the middle of the field towards your calling. In this case, they can't smell you as the wind is blowing your scent away from them. If all goes well, you should have a nice shot opportunity. The only problem could be if coyotes circle well to the outside perimeter of the field to get down wind of the sound source. This is actually a common problem for hunters in the east who do not have a luxury of huge open areas to hunt.

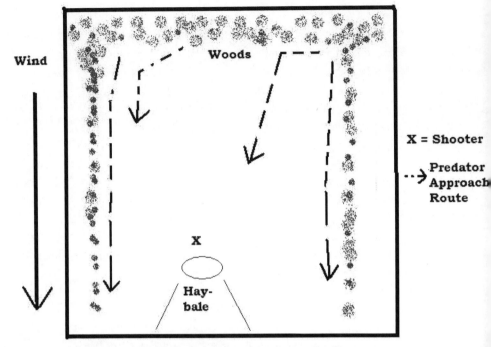

Fig. 1 Set up with wind in face

Let's look at the same scenario with the wind blowing at your back. In this situation, you are allowing coyotes to circle down wind of the sound source and you have a fine view of the area. The problem is… coyotes may catch your scent long before you see them enter the field or along a hedge row. They simply may not make it that far before sensing danger. If coyotes do appear in the field, as described in our virtual hunt, the hunter needs to shoot them before they get in side of the hunter's "Scent column." This is the area that, due to wind direction, is most likely to contain the hunter's odor.

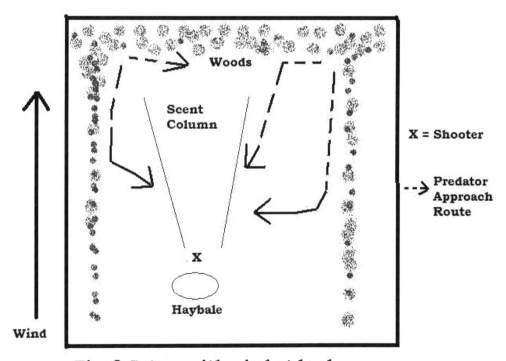

Fig. 2 Set up with wind at back

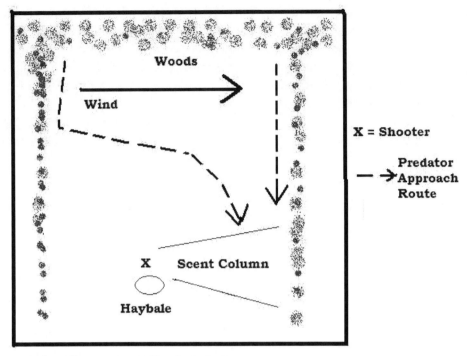

Fig. 3 Cross Wind Set Up

The wisest bet may be to set up using a cross wind in your favor. In our hillside hunt, let's pretend the wind is blowing left to right as you look at the field. Concentrate attention to the right side of the field, as most coyotes will circle here to approach. Now the right-side hedge row should be the coyote's best route which will allow him security and access to the sound. Due to the wind direction, you should have plenty of shooting opportunities before he enters your scent column.

Besides playing the wind, there are other aspects of setting up that are vital. When selecting a setup site it is important to be concealed, but not to the point that you cannot take a comfortable shot. If you are sitting deep inside of brush or tall grass, your vision may be impaired and you may miss seeing approaching coyotes until it is too late. Additionally, you may have difficulty maneuvering your firearm if you have obstructions around you.

Try to sit out of direct sun light. Find shadows and shade from any available source such as trees, bushes, farm equipment, or a hillside. The shade will enhance your camouflage efforts and coyotes will be less likely to spot you. Be sure that your outline is broken up, and you blend into your surrounding with proper camouflage from head to toe.

It is almost always advantageous to set up so that you can see the predators approach you from a distance. This will allow you to make any adjustments to get off a comfortable and confident shot. Position yourself near high elevations in the landscape, as in our virtual hunt, but be careful not to sit on the skyline. Get below it and use available vegetation to mask your presence.

The information presented thus far includes the essentials of proper setup. These essentials are so important that we will examine them further throughout the chapters in the book.

Taking the Shot

When the moment of truth arrives, the hunter needs to be ready to seal the deal. Anticipate where the predator will approach, and have the gun up and ready in that general direction. Shooting sticks will assist the hunter in doing so. If a rifle or shotgun is moved too abruptly, the sharp eyes of a coyote will have little difficulty picking up the motion. Shooting sticks will assist the hunter in this area. It is paramount that you know the effective range or your firearm, and have some idea of the distance of the approaching predator. It is a good idea to bring a range finder and get a fix on some landmarks ahead of time. There will be no time for range finders when the predator comes running in. The best time to shoot a predator is the first time he gives you the chance! So long as he is in your range, take the shot if it is clear and safe. It is advantageous to know that the actual vital target under all of that prime coyote fur is actually fairly small. The chest cavity is approximately six inches deep. Some folks wonder "where is the best place to aim on a coyote?" A broadside chest shot is always welcome and should be deadly.

If the predator is approaching too quickly and closely, "bark" at him with your mouth. They will almost always stop to investigate the sound. This technique works even after a missed shot. If, after you shoot, the predator spins like crazy, chamber another round and finish him off. Many times, coyotes will collect themselves and run off. They can go a long way, and the chase will not be fun.

If you score on the first shot, keep calling and perhaps another predator will be along shortly. A good technique here is to switch to a "ki-yi" or pup distress sound to lure in curious predators.

Weather Factors

As if there were not enough factors weighing in on success while calling predators, the issue of ideal weather conditions is also relevant to hunter success rates. Wind speed is a popular barometer of whether to go hunting or stay home. Fifteen miles per hour is the standard that most experienced callers use to make their choice. Wind speeds higher than fifteen mph make for tough calling conditions. High wind speeds simply mean that it is difficult for the predators to hear the call sounds. Unless you are competing in a contest, it may be best to save your calling efforts for a calmer night.

Hunting while it is snowing and raining is also difficult. As far as snow is concerned, it is hard to pick up any approaching predators in your scope that may come to the call. Additionally, most predators will be more inactive during a heavy snow so efforts to call should be postponed for a more opportune time. While hunting at night during a snow fall, it is nearly impossible to use lights effectively because of hunter's reduced visibility. Hunting in rain is almost never an enjoyable experience, and the toll that rain would have on your expensive equipment is enough to keep you inside.

Snow pack on the ground is another issue. It is helpful to have some snow on the ground for a variety of reasons. First off, it is easy to do some on-the-spot scouting by witnessing fresh tracks in the snow. Secondly, the presence of snow helps spotting incoming predators much easier, both during daylight and at nighttime. Additionally, a fair amount of snow on the ground makes hunting more difficult for the predators. They will have a harder time getting to small game prey. As a result, they are more apt to be hungry and respond more willingly to the distress calls. However, there is a point where too much snow is a hindrance. When snow levels are too deep, predators will move less because it is difficult for them to get through the snow and hence not come as readily to the call. When this is the case, possibly the best hunting strategy is to find snowmobile or farmer's tractor trails and hunt along them. All animals use these trails to help them through the snow and coyotes are no exception.

Air temperature considerations also merit some discussion. Since most predator calling is done in the winter, coldness is typically the issue. The basic question is ... How cold is too cold? The answer is ... As cold as the hunter can handle it! Predators will be on the move and be hungry in subzero temperatures. If the hunter is prepared for frigid temps and his equipment can perform the results may be worth the effort.

Let's include the topic of moon phase into our weather factors. As far as night hunting goes, some schools of thought favor a dark moonless night while others applaud a full moonlight night. The former believes that dark nights are better for calling because predators are less likely to spot hunters as they position themselves and/or equipment for the shot. Full moon advocates relish the fact that predators can be seen at great distances as they approach across the snow-covered ground. This author is a fan of a full moon for the above stated reason as well as the fact that it makes it possible to see through a regular scope without the use of lights for the shot. Moon phase is also paid attention to by hunters who only hunt during the daylight. They believe that predators that hunt all night on a moonlit night will be less apt to respond to calls as they have had success feeding and may be more restful during daylight than they would be on a dark (moonless) night.

The weather factors discussed above will certainly play part in the success of a hunt. If all the conditions are favorable, the odds of success will be in the hunter's favor. However, if hunters wait for all conditions to be perfect, he will drastically limit his hunting opportunities. In predator hunting, the terms "always" and "never" do not apply. The best time to get and call may be simply whenever you are able to do so. Calling in and killing a coyote in a 25-mph wind is possible and rewarding.

Hunting Pressure

When many hunters have called an area, it becomes tougher to successfully hunt the location. The uneducated predators will quickly fall victim to the efforts of hunters. Obviously, if they are killed, there will be fewer predators immediately available. If the predators are called in, but not killed, they will be difficult to call in again in that area.

One of the best ways to score in areas that are heavily hunted by others is to be the first person who hunts the area. Get the jump on the competition by calling in early fall. Another trick is to use calls that are non-traditional to the area. Do not use the standard rabbit distress calls; go ahead and try some different calling sequences such as using only howls or obscure distress sounds. It also may be a good choice to hunt the area very late at night. If the area involves a large tract of land, walk to remote sections where other hunters have not ventured. As we discussed earlier, it is getting hard to acquire hunting lands. If you must share areas with other hunters, be aware of these tips and you can still have success.

Predator Density

The number of coyotes living in an area will affect a hunter's success. It may seem obvious that areas that hold more predators will be more productive than areas that are host to only a few canines. The trick here is to gain access to as much land as possible. Then, keep logs of how many predators are seen on seasonal basis. As time goes by, the hunter will realize which areas are constant producers and concentrate on these areas. So long as prey species remain present and human disturbance is not overwhelming, the predators should continue to use the same areas on a yearly basis.

Summary

Understanding the factors in this Chapter can definitely assist hunters in their efforts to becoming better predator callers. It may take many outings and hours to realize how these variables come into play while hunting, but at one time or another, they all do. It is important to realize that not all hunts go as planned. The unexpected seems to occur in predator hunting more often than not. So long as the hunter learns each time they are afield, and can use some of that lesson on another hunt, he will become a more efficient coyote caller.

To conclude this important chapter, I'll tell a story of perhaps the most thrilling hunt I've experienced in all my years of coyote calling. The story is laced with examples of the factors mentioned in this chapter. I won't point out the factors in the text. I'll leave it up to the reader to recognize all that went well during the story of the "New York State Triple Play" ...

Calling in and shooting an Eastern coyote is always a thrilling and rewarding feat. Each successful hunt should be celebrated and cherished as the ratio of empty stands to successful harvests is often skewed. This story recounts the single greatest hunt in my 24 years of calling coyotes.

A walk along an established ATV trail, and over a drumlin that bisects two agricultural fields, put me on this early October setup. It was best to make the trek in the dim light of early morning to avoid being spotted on the way in. On this morning, there was no noticeable wind, so my main goal was to simply arrive at the setup position as quickly and quietly as possible. My uneventful venture took a turn as I was only a few yards from my destination. An eerie growl came from only thirty feet away. In the early morning light, I could see a large coyote standing broadside and growling at me. Even in the dim light, I could see its magnificent coloration. "What a fine specimen," I thought to myself! The problem was that I had no cartridges loaded in my rifle! The coyote trotted off and out of view. As soon as this coyote disappeared, another coyote stepped into view. All I could do was watch as he, too, trotted out of view. At this point, I quickly dug into my pocket for a few rounds and loaded up. I crept up to the field and one coyote was still there, standing fifty feet away. Upon seeing me, he ran into the standing cornfield.

I realized that the coyotes were not dramatically spooked and proceeded to set out my Foxpro digital call and the accompanying Jack-in-the-Box decoy. I was set up overlooking a clover field with the call and decoy set out at sixty yards. The call sound selection was cottontail distress, and it played for less than a minute when a yellow colored coyote charged in from the end of the field. I could see right away that this was neither of the other coyotes that just moments earlier had given me the close encounter of the coyote kind.

This coyote headed straight for the decoy. He must have seen me prepare for the shot, because he locked up at ninety yards, sat on his haunches, and started to howl. I never let him finish. Instead, I anchored him on the spot! The telltale "Whump" was music to my ears. What a way to start the season! However, the story does not end there.

Knowing that the coyote family units had not yet dispersed, I let the call play on with hope of bagging a second dog. Seconds later, another coyote came out of the cornfield below me and raced towards the decoy. He was coming in quickly and I needed to "bark at him" to stop him for a shot. Sure enough, he froze, and the Remington 700 in .223 was true again! A second coyote was down.

My goal was achieved and my excitement was high. When I stood up to investigate the kills, a third coyote ran out of the same cornfield and approached the decoy. Again, I had to "bark" to make him stop, and he made the costly mistake. Even as I stood, shaking from the adrenaline rush, I was able to take an off-hand shot and kill the third coyote at a distance of eighty yards.

I sat back down to think about what had just happened. Calling in and shooting multiple coyotes is a rarity in my part of the country... and I had just done it on the first hunt of the season.

Three coyotes in three minutes is the Authors personal record!

Many hunters believe the using hand calls is the essence of the sport.

Chapter 6

Calling to Coyotes

For most hunters, the art of calling is what attracts them to the sport. Seeing the coyote come running in to the sound you emit is the essence of the hunt. In all actuality, of all the factors, including those just discussed in Chapter 5, calling may be the least important. A bad caller, who masters all the other factors, will shoot more coyotes than a great caller who is sloppy in all the other areas. That being said, there are calling techniques and strategies that will make hunters more successful. Call choice, volume, duration and sequences are all important when attempting to master the skills of effective calling. Each of these aspects of calling will be discussed in this Chapter. The Chapter will conclude with a detailed look at examples of proven calling setups.

Call choice is up to the individual hunter. It's a big decision as there are so many types of calls and sounds available to today's hunter. The premise of coyote calling using distress sounds is simple; if a predator is hungry or at least curious, he should investigate the sounds of a distressed animal. The issue here is having an array of sounds so that call-smart coyotes can be tricked into coming around. If all the local hunters are using cottontail distress, it may be a good move to use another call such as bird distress. Not sounding like everybody else may be just the ticket for success. Sometimes; the oddest sounds produce the best results. I once had a string of success while using only prairie dog distress call sounds on the Foxpro call. Mind you, I was hunting in New York State and there wasn't a prairie dog around for 1500 miles! The point is… the sounds you select need not be from an animal indigenous to the area you are hunting. The bottom line regarding call choice is to select sounds that you have confidence in using. When confidence is high, it is easier to stay alert, stay on stand and that usually results in success.

The general rule of thumb concerning call volume is to start calling using low volume. The idea here is that any coyotes that are in the immediate vicinity will not spook at the sound of the call. If hunters start using too much volume, the nearby coyotes may be scared off by the unnatural loudness of the call. If no coyotes respond initially, volume can be increased accordingly. This theory seems like a safe choice.

The terrain and weather also plays part in call volume. If calling in areas that have steep hillsides, call volume may have to be increased to help sound travel. When calling smaller land acreage areas, call volume is best kept low so as to not blow out any proximate coyotes. Sound will travel farther on calm wind nights, so this needs to be considered. Use less volume on calm nights, at least initially. On the other hand, when dealing with the dreaded windy night, crank up the sound so that coyotes can hear you.

Call duration is another aspect of calling that needs attention. Actually, there are different viewpoints of how long to blow into a call or leave an electronic call on. A solid rule of thumb is to emit distress sounds for intervals of 30 seconds to 1 minute. When using mouth calls, you probably will want to stop after a minute, especially if you are putting a lot of emotion into your effort. If no coyotes appear after the first minute of calling, wait 2-3 minutes and call again. When using electronic calls, the sound can be played in the same fashion as if using a mouth call. However, many hunters, myself included, let the caller run continuously during the stand. Why is this? The belief is that coyotes, as they approach, may get distracted if they no longer hear the sound. If a coyote is locked on to the sound, it may be best to keep playing it until the coyote is dead on the ground. Call duration, like call choice, is an issue of hunter confidence. Find what works for you and go for it. However, it is also a great idea to stay flexible in your efforts to achieve success when all else fails. Do not repeat calling tactics that are productive. Just because they worked once does not mean they will work all the time. Experiment with calling duration until you find what coyotes are responding to. It is also best to remember that what works one day, may not work the next. Again, the hunter must stay flexible in calling strategies!

Wear gloves to hide the motion of your hands while using mouth calls.

Calling sequences are ways that hunters can be creative in developing scenarios in which distress or howling may occur in the wild. The most basic sequence is the before mentioned: 1 minute of distress followed by 2/3 minutes of silence and repeat. This is time tested and certainly will pay off. In fact, some hunters use it all the time and will not stray from using it. However, when no coyotes appear, it is nice to have some other tricks up your sleeve. Here are some examples of proven calling sequences…

<u>Squeak first:</u> Here is a basic technique that works great all season long. It's really a matter of simplicity at its finest. Begin each setup by using either a bulb squeaker or a mouth blown squeaker (Knight & Hales Rodent Squeaker is highly recommended). Again, use the squeaker for up to 1 minute, rest 2-3 minutes and repeat for up to 10 minutes. If

nothing responds, then switch to a rabbit distress call for the remainder of the setup. Don't be surprised if you never get the rabbit distress out as the squeaker is a highly-underrated call.

"THE" Sequence: Mike Dillon, of Foxpro Game Calls, gets credit for this magical sequence. I learned it as we hunted together during a fall filming session. The sequence was responsible for eyes to appear at every setup, all night long. It surely made a believer out of me, and I used it on subsequent hunts all season long. The sequence calls for the playing of three distinct sounds, each played continuously for 5 minutes, and in a certain order. The sounds in order are DSG Cottontail, Baby Cottontail, and Gray Fox Distress. For the first two sounds, the volume should be started low for the first minute and then increased to mid-range. The third sound can be played at mid-range initially

Dinner Party Call: No frills here, just a simple calling sequence that involves both distress and howling. Start off with a lone howl and follow with distress calls. Other coyotes may investigate the situation with hopes of getting in on the feeding action.

Gender Specific Howling: Calling coyotes using only howling is getting popular and here is a technique to increase success. Start with a locator howl such as a group serenade. If nothing answers, use a lone howl. At this point, it doesn't matter if you use a female or a male. In fact, use both alternately until you hear an answer. If all goes well, you will hear some response howling. Listen carefully and try to determine if you are hearing males or females. With experience, you will be able to differentiate between the alpha male and other coyotes. His sound will be deeper and stronger than the rest. If a male answers, and it is mating season, respond back with a female howl. You could also try some subordinate male howls. The territorial nature of the coyotes may cause the male to try to rid the subordinate males from the area. If a female answers, respond back with male howls. If she does not come to howls, go ahead and try some pup distress (even in winter) as her maternal instincts may cause her to investigate. While there is a legion of hunters who believe that coyotes really don't decipher between males and females, the above-mentioned howling sequences seem logical to me and I use them with success.

The sound of a coyote's howling is music to the hunter's ears

Calling Setups

Once you have determined what calls you are going to use, it will be time to make a calling setup. All of the factors discussed earlier come into play regarding making a setup. Indeed, the process requires thought, but fear not; it will become second nature as you gain experience. The type of setup you make is determined on your preferred style of hunting, type of firearm used and the type of terrain you have to hunt. Some areas may be large agricultural tracts that feature large cut fields. In this setting, a center fire rifle may be your best ally. Other locations may be mature hardwoods that feature valleys and ridges. Here a shotgun may get the nod. Again, your choice is a matter of personal preference. Let's view a couple of sample setups for use in each scenario.

Open Field Setup

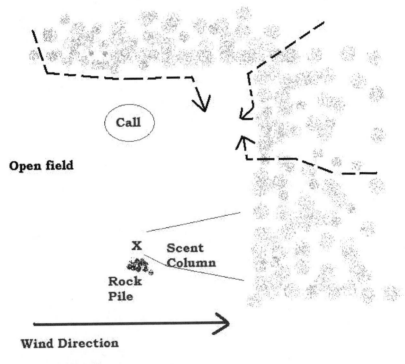

X= Shooter
- - -> = Predator Approach Route

In this diagram, the setup position is a rock pile in the middle of a cut field. This type of setup is best made at early dawn, late dusk or at any time in the darkness of night. The remotely controlled e-call and decoy is positioned 60 -80 yards away. The important thing to notice is that the position of the call allows for a coyote to approach the sound source, without detecting the scent of the hunter who is safely positioned thanks to the cross wind. If you realize that the coyotes are not committing into the open for shot opportunities while using any open field setup, you will need to alter your setup, such as in the hard woods.

Hard Woods Setup

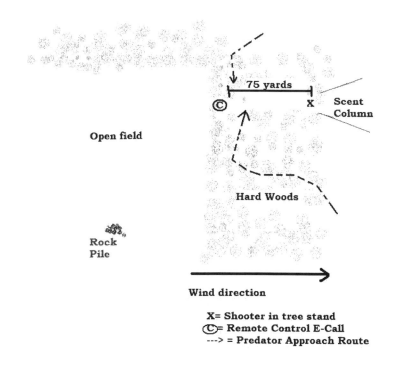

X= Shooter in tree stand
Ⓒ= Remote Control E-Call
---> = Predator Approach Route

Here is the same location, except this time, we wish to hunt by sitting in the hardwoods. Early to mid-mornings and late afternoons are optimal times to use this setup. I'm not keen on setting up in the woods at night. The setup position could be against a tree or actually up in a tree stand. The tree stand is a nice option because it puts the hunters scent up in the air and it also allows for a great field of vision for incoming coyotes. Once again, we are using a remote-controlled e-call and it should be positioned up wind. A wise choice is to place the call near the edge of the woods. Approaching coyotes who normally would not feel secure travelling into the open field will use the cover of the woods to investigate the sound. As they move downwind of the call, they should present themselves for a fine shooting opportunity.

To the Next Level: The Winner's Secret

My passion of coyote calling led me to host the Western New York Predator Hunt. The hunt is held each January and attracts over 100 2-man teams. Each year, there is a certain team that places in the top three and usually the takes first place. At the check-in, curious hunters pick the team's brains to find out how they consistently score on Eastern coyotes. They eventually let the cat out of the bag and shared their technique. The two-tiered technique relies upon a bona fide setup strategy and a unique calling sequence.

The theory behind the setup strategy is that Eastern coyotes will approach only when, and where, they feel safe and secure. This typically means along brushy hedgerows, wood edges and high grass areas. The hunters set up so that the prevailing wind blows into these types of areas. An e-caller is set out so that the coyote moves down wind of the sound source and is able to travel in the areas where they feel secure. One of the hunters is positioned nearby so they can intercept the coyote as he sneaks in.

The call sequence is unique in that it calls for a certain sound to be played at a very low volume while a second sound is played loud and over the top of the other. The low volume sound is the gray pup distress or a bird distress. The louder sound is a cottontail rabbit distress sound. When a coyote appears, the loud sound is stopped and the coyote is left to find the lower volume sound.

This technique can be done with a partner or a single hunter when using a remotely controlled digital caller. It is a technique that has merit and can be attempted whenever you feel as if you need to change your calling strategies.

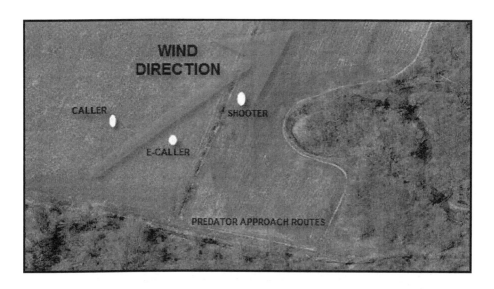

This picture illustrates how to pull off the "Winner's Secret."

Here is another view showing the hunters position and the coyote approach route.

The key to killing Eastern coyotes is to create realistic calling scenarios.

Chapter 7

Be a Storyteller

As we go through this chapter, let's assume that you have been bitten by the coyote calling bug. Whether you have been calling for 2 months or 20 years, you've accepted the honor of calling yourself a die-hard coyote caller. If so, it's time to take your calling to a new level in a concept that I call "becoming a storyteller" – it's a state of mind that affects how you go about your coyote calling

To become a storyteller, the hunter must allow his calling efforts to go beyond blowing a distress call for thirty seconds, resting and repeating. The hunter will create scenes, using combinations of sights and sounds, that will prove to be affective at attracting coyotes and keeping hunters motivated in their calling attempts. This may be especially important in areas that receive a lot of hunting pressure, and also late in the calling season when the calling response generally decreases. By late season, many coyotes have been subjected to all sorts of calling attempts. Don't forget with the expansion of our sport, you are probably not the only hunter trying to call coyotes in your area.

By creating a scene, calling sequences should tell an audible story so enticing that all coyotes within hearing range must investigate the call. Many times, two distinct call sounds are used in the calling sequence. For example, the sounds of a coyote eating a rabbit can be performed in concert. This can be achieved in two manners. First, is through the use of mouth calls. Performing different sounds is certainly possible and the market is full of diverse calls these days. While it is possible for a solo hunter to create the call sounds, it may be advantageous to have a partner with you to share the calling duties. One hunter can operate the rabbit call while the other does his best to emit coyote barks, yips and other sounds to signal that a coyote is about to dine on rabbit. Calling in a coyote under these circumstances could be considered the ultimate tag team experience.

The second way to produce multiple sounds is by using an electronic call. Today's digital calls are invaluable tools for becoming a storyteller. Between the hundreds of commercial sounds available, and those that hunters can record themselves and download to electronic callers, there is an endless supply of wildlife sounds. These sounds, when put together, can help create any situation that could occur in nature. The use of electronic callers allows hunters to switch sounds at the push of a button. It is also possible to mix the sounds and have them play on one sound loop. Storytelling doesn't get much easier than that!

Use Some Props

What's a good story without some characters? In addition to the sounds emitted, creating a scene involves providing some visual stimuli to the setup. The key to creating a scene is to allow incoming coyotes the opportunity to *see* what is happening in addition to what they hear. Coyotes are, in large part, visual hunters. A coyote that responds to the sound of an animal is distress may cease its approach if it does not get visual conformation that what they hear is real. If a sound is playing from a field and there is nothing to be seen in the field, suspicion may arise. Hence, the coyote may vacate the area before a quality shot opportunity occurs and that is not what we, as hunters, want to occur. The use of decoys adds realism to the situation. Just like sounds, there are many decoys available to hunters today. Rabbit, bird, and coyote shaped decoys are popular and can be found in many sporting goods stores. Old taxidermy mounts also work well and should not be overlooked as effective decoys.

Set your decoys in the open where coyotes can easily see them.

Setting the Stage

Be sure to set the decoys in an area where they can be seen by approaching coyotes. Most importantly, set up in a location where you can see the approaching coyotes and get a shot off. The coyotes will use wind to their advantage and attempt to circle downwind of the decoy and call spread. Allow yourself a view of the down-wind area and take the shot before the predator get into your scent column. It may be beneficial to add a misting scent as a final measure to the scenario. Although misting is an often-misunderstood concept in predator calling, many hunters believe that it can tip the scales of success in the favor of the hunter as far as getting a shot off. The addition of mist scent (typically a mixture of coyote urine, rabbit urine & water) to the setup can now appeal to three of the coyote's senses. Coyotes investigate setups as a result of the sounds and sights they encounter. The misting scent may be the icing on the cake as they approach the setup. The mist seems to create a state of confusion for coyotes and it is during this time that hunters can take a quality shot. This sort of trickery may just be what is necessary to fool cagey coyotes.

Famous fables

Part of the allure of becoming a storyteller is that it is a sure-fire way to beat the monotony of using only standard rabbit distress sounds. This may be just as important as calling in coyotes. When calling becomes tedious, part of the thrill of predator calling is obviously missing. By creating imaginative scenarios, hunters can stay fresh in their calling efforts. With this in mind, let's examine some proven calling scenarios.

"Predator & Prey": This sequence mimics the terror of a coyote attacking a prey species such as a rabbit or a fox. Creating this scenario calls for aggressive sounds that are best achieved by using electronic calls. The Foxpro
sound library contains several sounds that are available to listen to on their website. One of my favorites is the coyote and rabbit fight. It features the realistic gnashing of canine teeth coupled with the frantic screams of a dying rabbit. By playing this sound, and having a coyote and rabbit decoy nearby, you are telling area coyotes that one of their peers is having a feast and they are missing out. A truly unique scenario is the coyote and fox fight. Again, this sound is available through Foxpro and is highly effective at bringing in coyotes. The coyote's contempt for fox and their unwillingness to share the same area makes for a realistic scenario. I place a Lone Howler decoy and a mounted red fox toward each other in this situation. The call is placed right between them.

"Fawn caught in a fence": The intent of this scenario is to replicate the trauma of a fawn deer that has been caught in a barbwire fence. This sound can be replicated with the use of a simple deer bleat call. The real trick is to set up along a barb wire fence and hit the fence with your free hand (or a foot) while making fawn bawls and exaggerated bleats. The sound of the fence vibration will carry for hundreds of yards and adds realism to the situation. One word of caution when using this technique at night should be mentioned. Be sure to positively identify your target because curious deer will quickly approach the commotion of your call. No predator hunter wants to shoot a non-target species.

"Just add birds": The presence of birds in a calling setup is a blessing. Whether it happens naturally or if a hunter uses bird decoys, birds can be a hunter's ally. Alert hunters should notice birds that fly into a setup. Many times, they are actually following a coyote into the ruckus so that they may cash in on a free meal. The opposite is also true. Coyotes will be attracted to the commotion that birds provide. The presence of birds or bird decoys surely adds realism to the scene. A neat trick is to use crow sounds to attract crows before you start to use your traditional distress or howling sounds. Having a murder of crows circling above and cawing like crazy will definitely enhance your setup.

Hunters should be willing to adapt in their calling approach if they wish to continue to enjoy the sport. The concept of "Being a Storyteller" is one way to use a productive and exciting calling scenario. Next time you go out calling, do so with emotion and creativity. The examples mentioned here have proven effective. However, they are only three scenarios that could be used. Take your calling to the next level by developing some scenarios of your own. The end result will be a great sense of satisfaction when you trick an Eastern coyote into coming to a scenario that you created.

The coyote and fox fight scenario is one of the author's favorites for duping educated coyotes.

Coyote pup distress cries and the Lone Howler decoy are a deadly combination.

Night time is the right time for scoring on wary Eastern coyotes!

Chapter 8

Bring on the Night

Where permissible by law, nocturnal hunting can offer outstanding action. This is not to say that coyote calling in the pitch dark is easy. There are many considerations and tricks of the trade that go into a successful night hunt. In this chapter, we shall examine how to become a better nighttime predator caller. Some readers may be asking... "Why hunt at night?" Surely, this is a valid question and an analysis of a list of disadvantages and advantages may assist hunters in deciding if they wish to pursue predators at night.

Disadvantages/Advantages of Hunting at Night

Night hunting disadvantages include:

- The hunter's vision is limited and the predators cannot be as easily spotted as they approach.
- The gear necessary for night hunting is often cumbersome and awkward to carry afield.
- The actual shot is more difficult; the target is more difficult to see.

One the other hand, there are some definite advantages of night hunting:

- You are hunting during the natural hunting/prowling time of coyotes. They will be out looking for a meal and your calling is their "dinner bell."
- Coyotes will commit to open fields more easily at night and this makes for a fine shot opportunity.
- Hunting pressure from humans is normally lower at night.
- Winds are often lower at night.

- On a nice weather night, it's simply a great time to be afield.

If, after weighing the pros and cons, you are intrigued by the allure of night hunting, and don't mind missing your favorite TV show, night hunting may be worth your while. Welcome yourself to a new dimension of coyote calling!

Know the Law

Before you head into the darkness to begin your new adventures, be sure to have a thorough understanding of your state's laws regarding hunting at night. Each state has its own rules and the rules can be complicated. The laws regarding which caliber can be used fluctuate not only from state to state, but from county to county. Furthermore, some state's rules fluctuate during open deer seasons. By sure to obtain your state's game syllabus and have a complete understanding of the laws. If you are confused after reading the printed rules, by all means, contact your game department and ask an official to clarify any questions you have. There is never a good time to be caught doing something illegal.

Equipment for the Night Hunter

Coyote callers who wish to try night hunting can use their daytime gear with success. Camouflage is still important at night and hunters must make every effort to blend in with their surroundings. Accessories such as stools, shooting sticks are advised as the shot in the darkness is often tricky.

There is one additional item that will be invaluable for nighttime hunting...a spotlight! Where permissible by law, the use of lights will help hunters detect predators as they approach the setup. Without lights, the hunter must rely upon bright moonlight and a blanket of snow on the ground. There are many styles of lights to choose from and the choice depends upon style of hunting and financial resources. Some hunters simply tape a flashlight to their gun while others use a specialized spotlight that affixes to their scope. There are even types of lights are worn on the hunter's head. Hunters should experiment with different styles of lights and see which type best fits their hunting style. Variables to be considered will include weight of the light system, brightness of beam, ease of use, hours of operating time per charge and cost of the system.

One thing is common with these spotlight systems is the use of a red filter over the lens. Due to biological makeup of the canine eye, coyotes do not see the color red as red. This explains why they do not seem to be as bothered by the red glow of light and will continue their approach toward the hunter. On the other hand, when white light is used, predators tend to get spooked more often and vacate the area. Although it may be a question of the intensity of the light color, it's a safe bet to use a red lens cover in order to get a quality shot opportunity at predators at night.

I conducted an experiment on the topic of red vs. white light. My findings supported the use of a red lens for spot lighting and shooting coyotes at night. If other folks achieve success while using white light, I surely tip my hat to them and honor their opinions on the subject. One of the unique techniques in my experiment was to use additional intensity of red light just prior to shooting. This additional light was achieved through two methods. One was to have a partner turn on his spotlight just before the shot was taken. The other technique is to control the light intensity through the rheostat on the light system. This technique is recommended when hunting solo and requires a light system similar to what is found on Lightforce light systems. Either way, the additional red light allowed for the entire coyote to be illuminated and, hence, an easier shot opportunity occurred.

At the Next Level: Evolution of the Hunting Light

It is often difficult to select lighting systems that are both effective and efficient to use for night hunting. Criteria for making an educated decision include; spotlight brightness and range, battery life, weight of light system, ease of use and, of course, cost. When I think back through the span of my night hunting career, a memorable list of spotlighting gear comes to mind.

My first purchase was the Optronics 250 scope mounted light. This lightweight unit operated from a 6-volt battery and was sufficient for most of my nocturnal shots. I "upgraded" to the 350 model a few years later and found the light to be sufficient as well. These types of light systems were only used for the shot at the coyote. Scanning duties were appointed to 1 million candle power hand held spot lights, which were equipped with red lens covers. These powerful spotlights were terrific for picking up the reflective eyes at great distances. The problem was that their battery life was low, especially during cold winter nights. It was not uncommon to bring five or six lights along in the truck for a night of hunting. After years of endless recharging - which took up most available sockets in the house - and replacing broken triggers, it was time for a change.

A combination of hand held spotlights and an Optronics scope mounted light was my preferred method of operation in the early days.

My next purchase was the coveted Lightforce spotlight. This spotlight provided 500,000 candle power as powered by a 12-volt battery. Initially, the batteries would last six to seven hours a night. By using a charger in the truck, battery life could be extended to last all night. The Lightforce provided added convenience of being able to scan with the hand-held light and then quickly and quietly slip the light on the scope for the shot. One drawback of the system was the weight of the battery – a whopping five pounds! That gets heavy through the course of a night.

LED flashlights made a big impact on the predator hunting industry in recent years. Hunters could now say "Good bye" to heavy batteries and bulky lights. There are many styles, from many manufacturers, on the market today. All of the LED flashlight shooting and scanning lights offer hunters the ability to detect predator eyes from multiple hundreds of years in the distance. Furthermore, they illuminate the predators so much that it is possible to take reliable body shots from 200 to 300 yards away! The batteries, typically 18650's, last for hours and can be easily switched out in seconds.

Just when hunters had thought they had achieved illumination bliss, the use of night vision and thermal imaging scopes took hold. Although pricey, many hunters use these systems with great success and consider them "game changers" when it comes to night hunting success.

LED scanning lights make detecting coyotes possible

Nighttime Strategies

Pick a Good Night

Once you are armed with the knowledge of law, and with proper equipment, you are ready to head into the night. To maximize success, be sure to pick a good night to call. As discussed in the weather factors section of Chapter 6, all nights are not created equal and hunting during adverse conditions can do more harm than good. To reiterate, the first consideration is wind speed. Unless you are in a calling competition/hunt, save your efforts for when the wind speed is below 15 mph. In high winds, the sounds of the calls do not carry and the predators simply will not hear the call. As a result, predator response will be greatly reduced. This can lead to hunter dissatisfaction and that is clearly not our goal.

Snow is another consideration for nighttime hunters. A blanket of snow on the ground makes it easier for hunters to see coyotes approach. Too much snow, however, is rarely a good thing for coyote hunters. Deep snow makes travel difficult for both the hunter and the quarry and that simply equates to a tough calling conditions. Calling at night while it is actually snowing is also tricky business. If only a few flakes are falling, things will be all right. However, if the snow is coming down at a steady rate, it becomes difficult to see the reflective eyes of a predator. Additionally, the moisture associated with snow makes it hard to see through rifle scopes and is potentially harmful to spotlights.

The moon phase is a topic of great debate among night-time coyote callers. Some folks like a dark night with no moon, while others enjoy calling during full moon. Advocates for dark nights report that they can see the coyote's eyes more easily while spotlighting during a dark night. Furthermore, the hunters themselves are easier concealed on a dark night and they can get away with more movement. Hunters who favor hunting on a full moon night state that they can see coyotes as they make their way across a snow-covered field and that shots are easier to make in the moonlight. My personal hunting logs show positive results under both conditions and I welcome both scenarios. The fact is that I will be hunting on both dark and moonlit nights so I enjoy each type of evening while I am afield.

Setup

The approach to your calling location is just as critical at night as it is during day time hunts. Here is a piece of important advice... Always scan the field with your spotlight *before* you walk into it to set up! Many times, coyotes will already be in the field searching for food. As you scan, you may see the reflective eyes of an animal. If this occurs, stop immediately, set up and attempt to call in the animal. Analyze the eyes and movement of the animal to assess what you are watching. Often times the eyes are that of a deer. Once you determine that the eyes are those of a coyote emit squeaks on a call or with your lips. Many times, this is sufficient to call the coyote to you. A recent hunt shows the importance of pre-scanning the field as you approach a setup.

This mid-winter night hunt had me hopping from farm to farm. I would call for twenty minutes at each location and skip from farm to farm. Being a weekend, I was prepared to call all night if the weather permitted. The first farm yielded no action. No eyes, no howling in the distance. It was a classic empty stand. Undeterred, I drove to the next farm on my mapped-out route.

After a stealth-like roadside park job, I slipped over an embankment and scanned the large field with my Lightforce spotlight. As a panned from right to left, I picked up eyes on the end of my sweep. Instantly, I knew I was looking at a coyote! His reflective eyes were unmistakable and I sprang into action. I quietly adjusted my bi-pod to the maximum extension. This allows me to shoot standing up in a position that I call "Safari Style." Once ready, I positioned my rifle and attempted to find the coyote in the darkness.

Sure enough, he had moved in attempt to leave the scene. He must not have been overly concerned as he was still well within shooting range. I squeaked a couple of times on the bulb squeaker that is affixed to the bi-pod. This was enough to stop and turn the coyote broadside. He was fully lit up in the red glow of the spotlight and I took aim at his chest. The crack of the center fire interrupted the stillness of the night and the coyote fell in his tracks.

If no eyes are seen after you "Pre-Scan" the field, it is time to finish your approach and engage in a night hunt. Pay attention to the wind direction. Approach an area so that your scent does not blow into the area you wish to call a predator from. Additionally, be sure not to walk through areas that you suspect may hold predators. Doing so may cause you to bump roaming coyotes from the area. Move with stealth-like precision to your desired calling position.

It will be advantageous to call from an elevated location in the terrain. This will allow for a good view of any approaching coyotes. At night, you may lose sight of the eyes as coyotes move across the landscape. Dips, knolls, brushy spots, all make it difficult to track the motion of a responding song dog. By being positioned high in the terrain, you can minimize some of these obstructions.

Of course, attention needs to be paid to wind direction during the calling session. Be sure to allow yourself a view of the downwind area. Even at night, coyotes use their nose to assess the situation as they respond.

Calls of the Night

While making distress sounds, the hunter actually becomes the hunted. Coyotes will approach expecting to find a meal. As they approach the sound source at night, their forward-facing eyes, reflect the hunters light and appear red to the hunter (when using a red lens). When using mouth blown calls, it will be easy for hunters to detect incoming coyotes at night. The question arises... How effective are remotely controlled electronic calls at night? Early in my calling career, I would refrain from placing my electronic call far away from me for fear that I would not be able to see the coyote's eyes.

Recent experimentation has proved otherwise. When the call is placed out at distances of 40 -80 yards, it is still possible to see the coyotes approach. Furthermore, the combination strategically placed of remotely controlled calls and wind direction has improved my nocturnal success. By setting up downwind of the call, I have had numerous coyotes "walk right into my lap" as they circle in attempt to wind the call. This scenario presents a quality shot opportunity. Another benefit of using the remotely placed call is that it allows the hunter to make slight adjustments in shooting stance while the predator's attention is on the call source. Indeed, today's highly popular electronic calls have merit for night time use.

The Use of Lights

As mentioned earlier, it will be to your advantage to use spot lights when permissible by law. Be sure to have to light on during the entire calling sequence and scan the area as you call. Move the light at a steady rate of speed to cover the entire field of vision and after one sweep, go right back and re-scan the area. It is amazing how the coyotes can appear in an area that was just covered by the sweeping light beam. Keep scanning even after calling as coyotes can arrive at any moment. If eyes are detected in the beam of the light, keep the light on. If lights are turned off and on, a coyote will likely become alarmed and vacate the area. Aim the light so that the bottom edge of the light beam is positioned on the eyes. This is commonly referred to as "keeping them in the halo" of the light. The reason for doing so is that the full intensity of the light will not be on the eyes and the likelihood spooking the coyote, by lighting up his surroundings, will be reduced. Remember, coyotes like to move when and where they feel secure. If you are lighting up the area around him, he may lose his security and retreat into the night.

Taking the Shot

With glowing eyes in front of you, your heart should be racing! This is the quintessence of a night hunt. In this adrenaline-filled state, the question arises... When to shoot? First off, positive identification of the target is a paramount. Experience will be the teacher for differentiating various animal species at night. Once you have determined that you are dealing with a coyote, you can read their behavior to assist your decision of when to shoot. If the eyes are getting larger in a hurry, the predator is bounding in and that is a good thing. For the moment, that coyote is committed to the call and should be within shooting range in short order. If the eyes stop moving, and you know the distance and are comfortable with it, take the shot. Depending upon your light, you may see only the eyes or the entire animal. If only the eyes are seen, but you are sure it's a coyote, take aim at the eyes. Do not try to judge where his body might be in relation to the eyes and take a shot. It would be pure luck to connect on such a shot. If you can't clearly see the body, you must shoot at the eyes. There are some folks who say that shooting at the eyes is not enough of a target. With practice, as discussed in Chapter 4 and confidence in your firearm, it can be achieved with great results.

If the animal is sufficiently illuminated, a shot at the chest is recommended. The kill zone on a predator is small and shooting at night is tricky. Take advantage of the largest target you can.

Many times, the coyote will not charge in, but rather "hold up" in the distance. If the eyes appear to blink on any off, the predator is turning his head. This usually means that it is looking at another coyote. You are now dealing with a pair (or more) and the excitement is multiplied. Stationary coyotes will often break their stance when the call choice is changed. A good bet is to use a coaxer sound such as lip squeaks or the subtle sound of kissing the back of your hand. The bulb squeaker attached to the shooting sticks is perfect in this situation.

If the coyote appears to be nestled in a hedge row, back in the woods or in a brushy area, refrain from taking the shot. When they are not in the open, there will surely be some sort of obstruction between the coyote and the shooter. The end result may be a disappointing miss. Instead of rushing a less than perfect shot, it will be better to wait out the situation and attempt to lure the coyote at least to the edge of the cover.

After the Shot

If your hunt has gone as planned, the telltale "Whump" will indicate that your nocturnal shot has connected. Don't jump up and celebrate just yet. Keep calling and see if another coyote is willing to come in. If after 15 minutes, nothing shows up, it will be time to collect your prize.

Sometimes the eyes of a downed critter will still reflect back in your light. If so, you are lucky. You can simply walk out and check out your kill. If not, you have the task of finding the critter in the dark. After you shoot, take note of any features in the terrain to act as a guide in finding the animal. If hunting with a partner, have him hold the spotlight in the area where you shot the predator. It may help to remove the red filter and search with aid of the white light. The presence of snow on the ground and a bright moon will assist your efforts. Carry a camera with you because night time pictures capture the moment as it actually occurred.

Here is some other advice... do not leave any hunting items, such as shooting sticks and stools, in random areas of a field as you search for a downed animal. As you move about, you will lose track of where you set your items and the search for them will waste time and be frustrating to say the least! Leave such items resting against established landmarks such as a lone tree in the field or a piece of farmer's equipment.

For hunters who are interested in calling in coyotes, the darkness of night has a lot to offer. Using the strategies discussed in this chapter will allow hunters to get a basic feel for how to go about pursuing predators at night. Calling at night is a form of hunting that is as thrilling as any other, and it's a safe bet that anyone who tries it will be back for more. You know that you are hooked when you wish away the day and can't wait to bring on the night!

At the Next Level: Do it all Night!

Once you find yourself addicted to night hunting, you will find yourself not wanting to go home on a perfect night. There will be nights when you hear and see coyotes at every stand. When this happens, it is hard to quit hunting. For the hunter who wishes to stay out and pull an "all-nighter" there are some considerations.

First off, you need to make sure you have plenty of spare batteries to get you through the night. LED flashlight batteries typically last two hours with regular use. I carry four or five extra batteries in a Ziploc bag and carry them in an interior pocket to keep them warm on a cold night. I have read that it is best to not fully drain the 18650 batteries. Instead, swap them out if you notice that your beam is losing too much intensity. Some LED flashlights have built in sensors that will cause the light to blink as a reminder to switch the batteries. The FireEye scanning light from Foxpro has excellent battery life. Hunters can expect to get two full nights of hunting in, before the light needs charging.

My Foxpro e-calls last all night on one charge so I do not worry about that. However, it is not a bad idea to carry extra batteries for e-calls, just in case. The last thing you want to have happen is for your e-call batteries to die on those perfect nights. Be prepared and keep extra batteries at your disposal!

Bring plenty of batteries for an all-night hunt!

It is an excellent idea to map out your hunting spots so that you are hitting the spots in a certain order. This will maximize actual hunting time and minimize driving time. This is especially important in these days of higher gas prices. Speaking of gas... be sure to have a full tank before you start hunting. Gas stations may close before midnight, and you do want to get in a bind as your vehicle runs low on gas at 3:00 AM.

Make sure that you are physically ready for an all-nighter. If at all possible, take a nap before you head out for the night. Bring snack food and beverages. Any food item that has carbohydrates will provide necessary energy and drinks with caffeine will provide a boost to get you through the night. If at any time, especially while driving, you feel extra sleepy, pull over and take a nap. The experience of a night hunt is supposed to be fun. There is no sense in pushing yourself to the brink of exhaustion.

One thing that can definitely help you get through the night is a good hunting partner! By good, I mean one who has the energy and drive to endure stand after stand – and one who stays positive while doing it! The last thing you need is a guy who is constantly yawning or complaining about being out for so long. That alone will ruin the night. Indeed, finding a compatible partner is like finding gold.

Whether it is contest time or just a perfect night to be out, for the hunter who is ready, hunting all night can be productive and rewarding. Follow the tips provided and you can enjoy marathon nocturnal calling ventures.

Being prepared, mentally and physically, can have you smiling at the end of a long night.

If this is your partner, you're going to get sleepy yourself.

Don't put your rifle away when the snow disappears. Coyotes will eagerly come to the call during early spring.

Chapter 9

Three Season Calling Techniques

Winter is the season that comes to mind when mentioning coyote calling. However, coyotes can be called in at any time of the year and calling during the fall and spring, when permissible by law, can be just as exciting as winter time hunts. In this Chapter, we will look at some of the benefits associated with hunting during each season, and view some specific techniques to use during each season.

Fall: Jump Start Your Season!

My partner and I settled down for our first predator hunt of the season thirty minutes prior to sundown. By design, our set up position allowed us a grand view overlooking a cut corn field. After only seven minutes of rodent distress sounds coming from our Foxpro digital call, a lone coyote approached from the woods below. The coyote's coat glistened in the sun, and I took time to admire the blend of brown, tan and white just before I anchored the coyote with a 55-grain ballistic tip from my trusty Remington 700 in .223. The shot was a lengthy 175 yards but after a summer of shooting at woodchucks with the same rifle, the opportunity at this coyote seemed like a chip shot!

I should mention that this hunt occurred on October 1st, the first official day of New York State's coyote season. Typically, the mention of coyote hunting brings visions of an eager coyote hustling his way across a snow-covered field as he zeroes in on the sound of a rabbit in distress. While winter-white calling conditions may be the essence of the sport, the best calling action may occur well before the snow flies. Let's examine the benefits of early season calling and explore tactics to be used during this time.

Early Season Benefits

From a biological standpoint, the greatest benefit for getting the jump on predators early is the fact that hunt-able predator populations are higher in the early fall than during any other time of the year. As winter approaches, the coyote population drops dramatically. According to recent studies, only 30%-40% of coyote pups survive their first year. Additionally, adult mortality has been found to be at 40%. Most of this mortality is attributed to human cause. Many of these deaths occur at the hands of deer hunters who happen to see coyotes pass by their deer stands. You need not be Einstein to figure out that the best opportunity to kill coyotes is when there are more coyotes around to be killed.

A second reason to get after the predators early is the fact that you will be calling to the uneducated dogs. Your first visits to any area should be your best bet to score as the predators have not yet been subject to hearing various distress sounds. The young dogs will more eager to approach your calling and that can make for some fast action. As time passes, the coyotes that have been bumped by hunters or shot at and missed are more likely to ignore the familiar dine of rabbit distress. At the very least they may take a more stealth-like approach to the setup and not present an opportune shot as they survey the situation from deeper inside brush and wooded areas.

Lower hunting pressure is a third benefit to early season calling and is related to the educated dogs just discussed. If you are making the first call sounds the coyote hears for the season, you stand to have higher success. Once other hunters start inundating an area, it simply becomes more difficult to call predators in. For this reason, you should attempt to be the first caller to visit a locale. If you have areas that you know other hunters have access to, it is a good idea to call there first.

Early Season Tactics

Early season success comes from thorough scouting and the utilization of bona fide hunting techniques. For starters, make use of available vegetation to mask your approach and to break up your outline while setting up. Pay attention to the wind while approaching so that your scent is not blowing into the area you wish to hunt. Additionally, make sure that you have a view of the down-wind area as coyotes frequently circle downwind of the call source in an attempt to verify the safety of the situation.

As far as call sound choice is concerned, early season callers can take advantage of many types of call sounds. A great tip is to use coyote pup distress in your repertoire of sounds. By using pup distress sounds, the hunter is relying upon the coyote's maternal and paternal instincts. Whether it be from a mouth blown call or digital source, the sound of young coyotes in trouble is often enough to bring older coyotes in on the run. Coyotes are always on the lookout for a meal and virtually all distress sounds can work in the fall. This is a great time to get familiar with the numerous sounds that are available on today's digital calls or get used to using a new mouth call.

Another solid early season tip is to keep calling after a successful shot. The coyote family packs have not yet broken up as the young have not dispersed and this leads to some exciting setups. It is not uncommon to have five or six coyotes come in at one time. If you are using a remotely placed call, and kill a coyote, let the call play on. Then, use a mouth call to emit coyote whines and ki-yi's in addition to the distress sound. This sound combination can create a frenzy effect that keeps the other coyotes racing in to investigate the area.

Many hunters save their howling efforts until mating season in January and February. Again, these hunters are missing out on some of great action that howling can produce. Think not in terms of howling for breeding purpose but rather in terms of territorial rights. Male coyotes do not tolerate transient coyotes in their areas and go to great lengths to rid them. Smart hunters should use this knowledge to their advantage. Start off a calling set with a subordinate male howl, wait a few minutes and repeat. Sit back and wait for approaching coyotes. Be on the alert because they don't always howl to let you know they are coming. Keep a keen eye and watch travel corridors such as laneways and hedgerows. If a coyote does announce his presence and distain with a challenge bark, answer right back with a challenge bark/howl of your own.   Day or night, you should be able to track his location by the sounds of his calling. Getting in a howling battle with a coyote is always a thrilling hunt!

Predator hunters often measure their calling success by their fur take by season's end. By realizing the benefits of early season calling and by using the techniques presented in this text, hunters will be well on their way to increasing their tally. This season, don't wait until deer season is over... call in the fall and get a jump start on your coyote season!

Winter: A Caller's Wonderland

Mother Nature gave me a perfect present... two inches of new snow to blanket the fields of my favorite farm. As I made my way to a hedgerow to set up, I could not help but notice the multiple coyote tracks along the farmer's tractor trail. Anticipation ran high for the early morning hunt and before the sun crested the hill, a pair of coyotes was spotted approaching the digital call that was offering the canines an easy breakfast. I found the largest dog in my scope and the 55-grain ballistic tip

found its mark. Despite my best efforts to lure the second coyote in with "ki-yi" sounds, the action was over. That's OK by me! It was a great hunt and a terrific way to start the New Year, for this hunt took place on New Year's Day! For most coyote callers, the winter months are the most common times to pursue coyotes. For good reason, the winter months offer plenty to attract hunters.

Winter Offerings

For sportsmen in many parts of the Northeast, the white-tailed deer is still the king of all game species. Most hunters still put most of their efforts into scoring deer to fill their freezers and perhaps put a trophy on their wall. Coyote calling efforts are frequently put on hold until after the deer season. When the deer season ends, the woods return to a more serene state, from the human perspective anyhow, and then it is a great time to get into some serious calling.

With snow on the ground, it is easy to do some on-the-spot scouting and check for coyote tracks in the snow. It is simple to see which areas are being visited most frequently and these are the areas to call to. Snow on the ground also makes it very easy to spot incoming predators. The coyote has an unbelievable ability to blend into many types of landscapes. However, he stands out against a blanket of snow and will appear almost black in low light conditions. Even at night, it is possible to see coyotes as they move across open fields.

Snow covered terrain makes it more difficult for coyotes to find food. Gone are the fruits and grasses that were once effortless to find. Snowy winter conditions mean that coyotes will have to spend more time finding food. That is good news for the coyote hunter. Since they will be on the prowl frequently to find valuable food for energy, they will be more susceptible to the sound of an easy meal. An animal in distress is music to a hungry coyote's ears and that is why they often come running hard to the call.

Winter Calling Tactics

An inch or two of snow on the ground is not enough to alter normal hunting procedures. However, when the snow-pack piles up to over ten or twelve inches, there are some strategies to put into use.

Coyotes, like most other animals, have a hard time walking in deep snow. Unless the snow is crusted over and they can move on top, coyotes will alter their travel routes. When attempting to call in deep snow situations, hunters should find areas that have snow mobile tracks. The tracks make it easier for the hunter to access a calling location and the coyotes will use the pathways to get around. It may be advantageous to obtain a snowmobile and make your own tracks near a swamp or woods edge where you know coyotes reside. By doing so, you can almost dictate where coyotes will appear as they respond to the call.

A neat tip for hunting in deep snow is to find stands of pine trees. These areas will often times have a near barren floor due to the thick canopy provided by the needled trees. This means good hunting for coyotes, and they will be in the pines for weeks on end. Hunters should concentrate their efforts near these areas for deep snow success.

Another hotspot for winter coyotes is frozen waterways. Frozen swamps, creeks and marshes provide excellent travel routes for coyotes. Cattails are excellent cover for prey and are favorite hunting spots for hungry coyotes. The only caveat is to be sure the frozen surface is solid enough to support your body weight. No coyote is worth putting yourself into a potentially dangerous situation. I knew of a few hunters who carry a spare fishing pole in their vehicle. When the ice thickness is questionable, they cast a weighted treble hook out to drag the downed coyote to the shore.

A coyote taken over snow is always an exciting hunt!

However, use caution when hunting these types of areas. Make sure that the ice is sufficiently frozen and thick to support your weight while setting up to call or while retrieving downed coyote. There is no sense in putting yourself in danger. Hunters who frequent these types of locations have been known to use a fishing pole with a treble hook to cast and retrieve their trophy.

Spring: March Madness

A feeling of comfort came over me as I made "one last stand" for the night. This feeling of ease stemmed from my thorough familiarity with both my nighttime hunting equipment and the farms that I was hunting. Even in complete darkness, I could operate the electronic call remote like I was playing a Stradivarius and I could navigate over fences and pass through hedgerows with catlike precision. It should be mentioned that this hunt was taking place in late March and I had been hunting with regularity for the past six months! Hunting gear that took "getting used to" back in October was now an extension of my body and difficult-to-traverse land features had now become a "walk in the park." As it turned out on that night, my comfort assisted me as I called in a coyote, and was able to make a successful shot at 90 yards. Although he was the only coyote of the night, I felt complete satisfaction in the hunt. New York State imposes a season on coyotes. It would be a long six months before I could again enjoy my passion in my home state. It is this passion that drives me to hunt up to the bitter end of the season. As I have found out in recent years, March is a terrific time to enjoy our sport of coyote calling.

The author admires a late season coyote that succumbed to his calling efforts.

March Offerings

Many folks think of March as the beginning of spring. The warming of days and increased sunlight adds a new dimension for predator callers who have fought the elements of a tough winter. After enduring months of freezing temperatures and knee-deep snow, it's simply enjoyable to get out and hunt in less demanding conditions.

With the melting of snow, it is now much easier to approach set up locations. The task of parking your vehicle is far less tedious as you no longer have to worry about getting stuck in a snow bank. Getting to your calling areas is less work as well. Calling locales that were too difficult to access in January can now be reached with ease. It's now time to set your snow shoes aside and enjoy a walk that does not challenge your every step. Along the way, you may be treated to finding a shed buck antler or catch a glimpse of a Tom turkey for the upcoming turkey season. From a standpoint of providing pure outdoor pleasure, March has a lot to offer. The list of benefits does not end here.

Operating calls, both mouth blown and electronic, becomes more convenient in March. No longer do you have to contend with calls "freezing up" in the middle of your sequence. Setting out remote controlled calls is far less tedious as you do not have to trudge the extra 50-60 yards in the thick blanket of snow. Hunters will quickly realize the joy of tasks such operating remote controls, loading your rifle and operating lights at night while wearing lighter weight gloves versus the thick gloves necessary for hunting in the dead of winter.

The batteries used to operate your hunting gear also get a break in March. Cold temperatures wreak havoc on battery life. When you add up the number of batteries in flashlights, calls, spot lights, decoys and video cameras it can get pretty costly and, more importantly, frustrating when batteries die at the most inopportune time.

Late Season Tactics

If the winter months have passed you by and your calling efforts have not yet been satisfied, don't put your gear away just yet. If your state laws permit, you may want to experience some March Madness for yourself. Here are some tactics and tips for scoring late season coyotes.

The most obvious strategy would be to try to find coyotes that have not been educated throughout the winter months. Hunting remote areas or areas that received no calling pressure can still pay off. As was mentioned earlier, the absence of winter's deep snow will allow hunters to access more land.
By walking to remote areas, you may be reaching animals that have not yet heard the allure of a hunter's call.

According to my hunting log, two types of calling scenarios account for most of my March coyotes. The first is a back-to-basics approach that relies on the "Less is more" principle. This simplified technique is a change from the rabbit distress sounds that coyotes have been bombarded with all season long. The idea is to use single coyote howls in conjunction with a rodent squeaker call. To accomplish this, I prefer the use of a mouth blown rodent call (Knight & Hale's Rodent Squeaker is highly recommended). Blow into the call as if it is a typical rabbit distress call. Stay on the call as long as your lungs permit. Normally, my duration for using the rodent distress is 30 seconds to 1 minute. While resting, scan for incoming critters. Then repeat the process 2 or 3 times.

If no coyotes come to the initial distress sound, emit a lone howl. Don't overdue your howling efforts. A simple howl will tell other coyotes that you are in the area. They may respond to defend territory, protect food sources or for lingering love interest. Don't expect the coyotes to answer back to your howls, although it would be nice. Be on the lookout, as they often approach silently. Repeat the rodent distress sequence and lone howl every ten-fifteen minutes and plan on making each set up last at least thirty-forty minutes. This simple calling strategy is a no-frills affair that can pay off in big ways.

The second calling scenario that proved deadly at this time of year involves the techniques covered in Chapter 7, "Be a Storyteller". By late season, the coyotes that are still roaming around have seen and heard it all. To kill them, you must pull out all the stops regarding set up and sound presentation.

If you truly enjoy predator calling, you will want to do it as often as possible. In most states, it is possible to enjoy calling in at least three of the four meteorological seasons. Within this text, I have provided the benefits of early spring hunting and shared some calling tactics that have proved productive for luring in coyotes. I would encourage all predator callers to not put their camouflage away when the snow disappears, but rather take advantage of the end of the season possibilities that March provides.

This coyote was killed during the second visit to a farm on the same night!

Chapter 10

Two Timing Coyotes

The cottontail distress call had only emitted for a few minutes before the red glowing eyes of a coyote reflected in the beam of my spotlight. A second pair of eyes appeared and the excitement was doubled. The pair of nocturnal hunters made a bee-line for the Foxpro call and I had a tough time figuring out which coyote I should be concentrating on. As they closed the distance to 60 yards, one coyote presented an opportune shot and my CZ .22 magnum was true again. A quick glance of my indigo watch indicated the time was 11:00 PM. With one coyote down, I maintained position and let the call play as I waited for the other dog to come back to check on the whereabouts of its mate. After fifteen minutes, and no visitors, my excitement overcame me and I ventured across the field to find a prime female red coyote.

Although this was my first night to hunt this newly acquired farm, it was not my first calling experience there. I had called from the exact same knoll in the field, using the same Foxpro cottontail distress sound only 2 hours prior! During the first hunt, which took place at 9:00 PM, I received no response to my calling efforts during a 30-minute set. This came as a surprise because the farmer had told me that no one else calls there and there were numerous predator tracks in the snow. I knew that I must return at some point to try again, the question was... When? Had I followed conventional predator hunting wisdom and not returned for a week or so, the exciting hunt at 11:00 PM would have not occurred.

This hunt and two successful others that occurred in the same week gave me new insight regarding how and when coyotes come to the call. I developed a theory on calling and predator response. My belief is that, assuming appropriate approach, setup and calling techniques are used, coyotes will respond and approach a hunters' calling ... *if the coyotes are in the area at the time of the calling*. If no coyotes are seen or heard, it means that they are not within hearing distance of the call at the time when the hunter is present. If a hunter experiences an "empty setup" does it mean that that particular farm is "no good"? Certainly not! It simply means that the coyotes were not in the area when the hunter was calling. My theory does recognize the fact that educated and over-called coyotes may buck the trend of anticipated response. All in all, however, the premise of the theory holds true.

Think about this scenario... Fresh snow has fallen and you are excited for an afternoon hunt. Despite your textbook setup and stellar calling, darkness falls and you still have not seen any coyotes. You vow to return in the morning, and when you do, the area is strewn with coyote prints. After 30 minutes of confident calling, the result is the same: No takers! The sign left by the coyotes tells us that were in the area at one point in the night. The old saying "You've got to be in the right place, at the right time" is never so true! Again, calling response will be greater when coyotes are in the immediate calling area at the same time as the caller.

Trail cameras are a solid tool for determining when predators are using an area. Most models have the ability to stamp the date and time right on the picture and you will have great evidence of the predator's presence in the area. Set a camera on an established travel route and check it after a week. Try to establish a pattern to the predator's movement and you will have an advantage when it comes time to call the location. Last season, I set my camera along a well-used ditch in a farmer's field. I noticed that all of the pictures were taken in the morning hours. While my nighttime calling sessions were fruitless, I bagged two coyotes during my first mornings while calling near the ditch. Indeed, the camera was invaluable as far as determining just when the coyotes were using the area.

Going Twice Around

During the fall of 2007 and winter of 2008, I employed a new strategy to increase my calling success. I started to re-visit farms two (sometimes three) times a night until I got a response from predators. A desire to test my theory on predator response and a desire to be more productive led to the twice around technique.

The first step in this technique is to map out the farms that you wish to hunt on a particular night. In this age of rising gas prices, it makes sense to take care in planning so that you are not driving farther than you need to. Arrange your calling spots in regions and develop a travel loop. It stands to reason that you will not be visiting all of your hunting locations every night. I assembled three calling loops for the farms in my hometown area. Each night that I hunt, I cover one loop and that allows the other regions to "rest" from my calling efforts. Since I live in the east and sometimes hunt suburban areas, I will visit certain farms early in the evening so that I am not hunting there in the "wee" hours of the night. It stands to reason that hunters should communicate with landowners so that they are aware that you may be hunting their land on a late-night shift, assign each farm a number and you will be ready to roll.

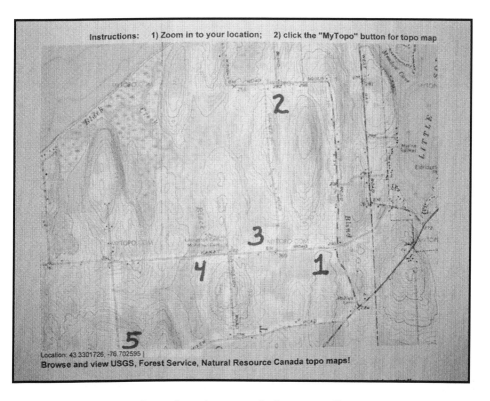

Create a map of your hunting spots before going "Twice Around."

Assuming that the wind conditions are ideal, set up and begin calling the first farm on the loop. Call using your preferred sequences and sounds and stay for one half hour. If no action is realized, pack up and travel the next farm. Take notice of tracks in the snow as you enter and exit each farm. Constant scouting and increased awareness of your environment can never be a bad thing for the astute predator hunter. Hopefully, as the night progresses and you make your way around your loop, you will have had some response to you calling efforts. If not, it is time to go twice around. It's time to give those same farms another dose of calling and see if any predators are now available to respond.

Depending upon the number of farms on your loop and when you started your hunt, you may be approaching late evening. The areas that you first called have received 1.5 to 3 hours of "rest" and it's time to pay return visits. Start your hunt over by re-visiting farm # 1 on your loop. I typically use the same setup location the second time around. Although changing things up may have merit, I pick my nocturnal setups based upon my ability to see incoming predators and, on the smaller eastern land tracts, one setup location seems sufficient for the entire farm. My records indicate that there is no need to change the call sound on subsequent visits. Call with confidence knowing that the predators were not in the area earlier and now may be with earshot of your best distress wails and cries.

Not All the Time

Although going twice around has proved to be a productive technique, I am not a supporter of using it too often in the same region. Frequent visits are the first step in burning out a spot. If a hunter were to use the twice around technique even once a week, I'd bet his calling success would diminish dramatically on any given farm or ranch. I specifically use the twice around technique during predator calling contests and on weekends. If I drive to a location 2 hours from my house and have six farms to hunt in that area, I will use the twice around technique and make a night of it. In the morning light, I will return to the farm where I heard the most howling or saw the most sign during the night. I typically make a one hour stand during the first hour of light and surrender for the day. By this time, it's time to charge batteries and spend time with the family.

    I frequently hear predator hunters say that they know coyotes are on their farms but they do not come to the call. They are astounded when they "do everything correctly" and still have no fur in their trucks. These are the hunters who could benefit from the twice around technique. Being in the right place at the right time is paramount for duping cagey coyotes. This technique helps put you there. If your predators are giving you the slip, try going twice around on them. You may be pleasantly surprised by the results!

This coyote was killed on the Author's fourth attempt at calling it in!

Chapter 11

Stubborn Coyotes

At least once a season, every hunter will come across a stubborn coyote. I'm talking about a coyote that refuses to go down the easy way. You may encounter him several times before either giving up on him or finally killing him. The "Gimpy" coyote was such a dog.

I acquired permission at a farm that featured a peculiar landscape – the field above the cow pasture had a convex formation. In order to gain any visibility, I had to position myself near the apex of the hill. Once in position, the view field of vision was adequate, but not a picture-perfect setting.

On the first night there, I bumped a coyote that was already in the field. I set up despite scaring off my quarry, and was treated to a series of coyote howling. I joined the vocal battle and we howled back and forth for 45 minutes. At times, I could see the coyote's eyes at the edge of the woods several hundred yards away. In desperation, I played Ernie Wilson's Death Cry sound on the Foxpro FX5. As I scanned with the handheld Lightforce spotlight, I saw the reflection of coyote eyes standing right next to the remotely placed call. How he got there without me noticing was a mystery. He was so close that I could see his entire body in the red glow of cast light. I noticed that he was limping with his rear left leg. I should have shot him at that precise moment, but he was about grab the call, and I was mesmerized by the show!

As it turned out, he caught my scent on the call and fled the scene. Yes, I kicked myself and broke one of my own rules: always shoot when you get the first good opportunity!

I returned to the same spot twice more, both at 11:00 PM, in the next two weeks only to find "gimpy" already in the field. He would instantly bolt when hit with the light. One these nights, we would not approach my calling or the glow of my spotlight. Clearly, I had to change things up to score this cagey dog.

I planned a morning daylight hunt for fourth trip. It proved to be a good decision as the hill top coyote attempted to slip, or should I say "gimp," along the woods edge to investigate some bird distress from the Foxpro. An easy eighty-yard shot put an end to the story at 7:00 AM!

The hunt involving the "gimpy" coyote proved an interesting point: Sometimes coyotes don't come charging to the call and your calling tactics may have to change in order to have success. Whether you have a day, a night, a week or even a season to score a stubborn coyote, it can be done.

Typically, stubborn coyotes are encountered later in the season. As discussed in Chapter 9, late season coyotes are often educated, and not willing to charge into calls like the younger, more naive coyotes of October. A stubborn coyote is one who likes to scold your presence in his neighborhood. If you hear repeated barking or challenge barking, you know you are dealing with coyote that isn't really ready to come in. He will take some work. Sometimes the howling isn't as threatening as a challenge bark. You may be listening to a coyote, or pack of coyotes, which are sounding off with lone or group howls, but not approaching.

The first thing to do is realize that you in a good situation for an Eastern coyote hunter... you are in the company of a coyote! Many hunters will leave the area if the coyotes do not appear after fifteen minutes. This is a big mistake! Here is my take on the situation: You know coyotes are in immediate area so why would you leave? That is like leaving a dance club full of pretty girls at 9:00 PM... *alone!* A better bet is to wait out the coyotes. Let your presence be known and then give them a dose of quiet. This is akin to getting quiet on a hung-up gobbler with hopes that the silence will break him and he will approach your setup. Your wait may be forty-five to sixty minutes, but if you get a shot, it will be well worth the wait.

If the coyote can be heard drifting away, you may have to resort to re-locating or giving up on him for the time being. If re-locating is possible, try to get ahead of where he was going and use a different prey sound. I must say that is it difficult for many Eastern coyote hunters to re-locate on mobile coyotes because many farms are not that large and the coyote could be onto new grounds in short order.

If you have given up on a coyote, do not feel that you won't be able to call him in during future visits. However, you may have to change your strategy somewhat. Stubborn coyotes still need to eat, mate and defend territory.

The first change-up may be to alter your calling position on the farm. Of course, this will be somewhat dictated by wind direction. If you can alter your setup location, you stand a chance at scoring that obstinate critter. Along these lines, changing your calling sounds will tip odds in your favor. If a coyote has heard your rabbit distress two or three mornings, send out some bird distress. You may want to switch from mouth calls to electronic calls and vice versa. While these are not huge tactical maneuvers, they may be enough to get the job done. As with the hill top coyote, a change in your time of calling may produce results.

If you have a coyote, or coyotes, that simply refuse the come to the call, you may have to entice them with bait. Where permissible by law, baiting is an effective way to kill coyotes. Baits are best when the coyotes are unable to carry them away. Road kill deer or buckets filled with frozen meat scraps work well. Although this book is geared towards the art of coyote calling, I mention baiting because it can be done in conjunction with calling. In fact, I wrote an article called "Bait and Pitch for Coyotes" in the August 2008 issue of *Predator Extreme* Magazine. I found that I was unable to sit for hours waiting for coyotes to approach my bait station. One night, I asked myself "Why not call over this bait?" I figured the calling would let other coyotes know that someone was invading their free meal. I went further by placing a fake coyote decoy near the bait. Despite the extra work involved, the technique is productive… especially for stubborn coyotes!

A "Baitsicle" will keep coyotes in the area so you can call to them.

If, in your coyote pursuits, you come across a coyote is not willing to cooperate, don't despair. Instead, alter your technique and you may trick him into making a costly mistake. Sometimes a coyote that you come to know provides you with challenging hunts is worth more alive than dead. He can teach you much by listening to his sounds and watching his behavior. Don't feel bad when you finally kill him, though. There will be more stubborn coyotes in your near future.

This coyote came into a lone howl performed near a bait site.

Be sure to take plenty of pictures of your hard-earned trophy coyote!

Chapter 12

After the Shot

A close friend of mine once said… "Hunting is anti-climactic after the trigger is pulled." To some extent this is true. However, after a successful Eastern coyote hunt, which results in a canine lying at your feet, the adrenaline continues to flow. After all, you have just killed one of the most alert and cautious predators on the face of the earth. At that moment, you also need to know what you are going to do with it. That decision is based upon your purposes for hunting coyotes in the first place. Some folks pursue coyotes to protect livestock while others do it to sell the hides to raise money. Surely, there are other reasons as well.

Fur harvesters are concerned with obtaining prime pelts and preparing them for fur buyers or to sell themselves at auctions. The process of skinning, fleshing and stretching is an art in itself. So much so, that there are many books that deal with that very subject alone. Hunters who wish to learn the skills necessary to become proficient at handling their own fur would be well advised to obtain a DVD that demonstrates the process thoroughly or tag along with an experienced individual as they prepare some fur. By doing so, the learning curve will be shortened dramatically.

Some folks desire to get their first nice coyote made into either a rug, pedestal mount, or even a full body mount. If that is the case, the coyote must be taken to the taxidermist as soon as possible. It has been my experience that the coyote hide "goes green" within a day unless temperatures are well below freezing. When a pelt is in this condition, many taxidermists do not like to work on them as the hair tends to slip.

No matter what you end up doing with your trophy, be sure to take plenty of pictures to capture the memory. Try to avoid the common picture showing the coyote in the back of the pickup or hanging in the garage. Do the animal some justice and take some nice pictures in the setting where it was killed. Pay attention to lighting, shadows and backgrounds. Also, take many pictures from different angles. Professional photographers take hundreds of photographs only to come up with one that appears perfect. You don't have to take that many, but you get the idea. In the digital picture age, this is quite possible to take many pictures without running up huge printing costs. Your pictures may have more value than serving as memories in your photo album. There are numerous online photo contests available and your pictures could end up winning you some nice prizes. These contests are typically free to enter and are another dimension of the fun of coyote calling.

A full body mount is an excellent way to commemorate the memories of an excellent hunt.

Gain information and motivation from the many publications available today.

Chapter 13

Hunter Resources

In penning this book, it was my original intention to provide a source of information that would help hunters gain an understanding of the Eastern coyote, and learn how to become successful at calling them in. I truly hope that as you read this final chapter you feel stronger in those areas. If you wish to be a true "student" of the Eastern coyote and to calling him, your desire to learn should not end here, however. One message that I often convey in my seminar presentations is that there is always something to be learned, whether it occurs in the field or in the pages of a magazine. Luckily for today's hunter, the coyote hunting segment of the hunting industry is growing by leaps and bounds. As a result, there are many sources of coyote hunting material available to assist eager coyote hunters, as well as to motivate experienced coyote killers.

Magazines & Books

In a time when electronic media seems to be all the rage, there is still something nice about simply sitting down and reading a magazine article or book on the topic of hunting. As coyote hunting gains popularity, most major outdoor magazines have realized the trend and offer seasonal articles to quench their reader's appetites. Coyote enthusiasts who long for more specific and thorough reading will appreciate the offerings of Grandview Media's *Predator Xtreme*, Krause Publication's *Predator Hunting* and The Varmint Hunter's Association's *Varmint Hunter* Magazine. All of these publications feature the latest techniques and information that is beneficial to coyote callers of all experience levels.

When I first got started in coyote calling, I wanted to absorb all that I could to become more successful. While at the local bookstore, I came across *Predator Calling* by Gerry Blair. I recognized Gerry's name from his articles and this was the first book that I read that pertained to the art of calling coyotes. It was spun with wit and information as only Gerry can do. In 2008, the book was re-published with new color photographs. It remains a "must read" for anyone who wishes to call himself a coyote hunter.

Internet Websites and Forums

Perhaps the quickest way to obtain any type information is on the internet. Coyote hunting information is no exception and there are some superb web sites devoted to calling coyotes. Perform a search on a browser, such as Google, and a plethora of sites will appear. The Grand Daddy of them all might be Predator Masters. This site, with its highly active forum, will allow its members to gain access to all things relative to coyote calling. It truly is a great site and community of hunters. Be advised, once you visit, you will be back for more. Probably more than you should. It's that addictive.

DVD's

There are many coyote hunting DVD's available these days. So many that we can't keep up! Most of the latest releases feature top notch filming, Hollywood-like editing, calling tips and plenty of action. When I watch coyote calling DVD's, I do so for two reasons. First is motivation. The sight of a coyote coming to the call, even on film, is enough to encourage me to get out and do some calling. The second thing I like to do when watching a coyote calling DVD is to watch the behavior of the coyote. It is informative to observe how coyotes react as they respond to hunters calling attempts. This being said, one DVD that I would like to mention here is entitled *Coyote Behavior* by Jay Nistetter. This DVD concentrates on coyote behavior as they approach. It speaks volumes on what to watch for as a coyote investigates your setup. Transfer the information that is on the DVD to what you see when a coyote comes to your calling and you will be a more successful hunter.

Calling/Hunting Seminars

Another sign that the sport of coyote hunting is increasing in popularity is the increase in the number of instructional calling seminars that are held around the country. I find that it is almost always beneficial to attend seminars because it is always nice to hear what other folks have to say about calling in coyotes. It is important to go into seminars with an open mind and not have a "know it all attitude" before the speaker starts his presentation. If one tidbit of information helps you kill a coyote, then attending the seminar was worthwhile.

Seminars are great places to learn new calling tricks.

Appendix A

The Coyote Calendar

Month	Ecology	Impact on Calling
January	Mating season begins	Howling can be an effective way to get response from coyotes
February	Mating continues	Same as above
March	Tail end of mating; Den preparation; Rubbing occurs on fur	Coyotes still respond to howling & distress calls. Many hunters cease hunting efforts.
April	Pups can be born and are in den	Most sport hunters let coyote parents tend to pups
May	Same as above	Same as above
June	Pup growth & exploration	Same as above
July	Continued pup growth & exploration	Same as above
August	Rendezvous activity	Same as above
September	Family units are still together	Fall hunting commences. Pup distress effective
October	Fall dispersal starts	Fall calling can produce multiple coyotes to respond at once.
November	Dispersal continues	Roaming coyotes more susceptible to calling
December	Coyotes begin searching for mates	Calling response is good when snow makes finding food more difficult

Appendix B

Coyote Contest Check List

Coyote hunting and calling contests are sprouting up all across the country. These events can be challenging as well as a lot of fun. Whether you enter to win or just to gain experience, you are sure create some lasting memories.

Here is a list of items that will make your contest participation more enjoyable…

- A full tank of gas in your vehicle
- Cash in case your bank card can't be read at a gas station
- A cell phone
- GPS to get you where you need to be
- Phone numbers of people who live in the area you are hunting, in case you get stuck
- Mouth calls in case your E-Call has malfunction
- Toilet paper
- Sufficient bullets
- Spare rifle or shotgun
- Tool kit
- First Aid Kit
- Snow shovel in case you get stuck while parking roadside
- Pull string to clear your barrel in case you drop it in the snow
- Multiple batteries for your spotlights
- Spare spotlight system in case of malfunction/breakage
- Flashlights
- Camera
- Snack food
- Beverage
- Tarp, garbage bag, rack or trailer to carry critters
- Multiple batteries for your flashlights, calls, and camera

Appendix C

Taxonomy of the Coyote

- Kingdom: Animalia (includes all living and extinct animals)
- Phylum: Chordata (animals with a single dorsal nerve cord)
- Subphylum: Vertebrata (animals with a spinal column)
- Superclass: Gnathostomata (all vertebrates with upper and lower jaws)
- Class: Mammalia (animals with mammary glands, hair, and middle ear bones)
- Subclass: Placentalia (animals with placenta)
- Order: Carnivora (meat eating animals)
- Family: Canidae (includes dogs, wolves, foxes, coyotes, and jackals)
- Genus: Canis (includes wolves, jackals, and coyotes)
- Species: latrans (scientific name for the coyote species)

About the Author

Andrew Lewand was born and raised in Fairport, New York, which is a suburb of Rochester. He is married, and has two children. He enjoys sports, and is a Physical Education teacher and lacrosse coach at Fairport Central Schools. Lewand is an ardent hunter who regularly pursues squirrel, deer, coyote, fox, woodchuck, crow, and turkey.

Lewand's fascination with coyotes began when he was a student at SUNY Cobleskill majoring in Fisheries & Wildlife Technology. Lewand began to intensely study the Eastern coyote and its biology. He then applied this knowledge to his hunting efforts, and the result was a highly effective way to hunt the coyote. 45 years later, Lewand still enjoys studying and pursuing the coyote and has formed The Bark at the Moon Coyote Club as a way to share the thrill of predator hunting. Lewand is a free lance writer whose work can be seen in many magazines as well as a frequent presenter of predator hunting seminars across the Northeast.

More Books by Andrew L. Lewand

Ordering information is available at...

www.barkatthemooncoyoteclub.com

Made in the USA
Middletown, DE
14 August 2017